PEACE

DATE DUE			

PEACE IN SEARCH OF MAKERS

Riverside Church
Reverse the Arms Race Convocation
Jane Rockman, Editor

Judson Press ® Valley Forge

PEACE IN SEARCH OF MAKERS

Copyright © 1979
Judson Press, Valley Forge, PA 19481
Third Printing, 1981

Unless otherwise indicated, Bible quotations in this volume are in accordance with the Revised Standard Version of the Bible, copyrighted 1946, 1952, 1971, 1973 © by the Division of Christian Education of the National Council of the Churches of Christ in the United States of America, and are used by permission.

Library of Congress Cataloging in Publication Data

Main entry under title:

Peace in search of makers.

   Addresses given at a convocation at the Riverside Church, New York, Dec. 4-5, 1978.
   Bibliography: p. 156
   1. Arms race—Addresses, essays, lectures. 2. Atomic weapons and disarmament—Addresses, essays, lectures. 3. Peace (Theology)—Addresses, essays, lectures. I. Rockman, Jane.
JX1974.P3697   327'.174   79-13105
ISBN 0-8170-0854-3

The name JUDSON PRESS is registered as a trademark in the U.S. Patent Office. Printed in the U.S.A. ⊕

Photo credits: pages 8, 21, 42, 46, 82, 96, 108, 123, 143, United Methodist Board of Global Ministries, by John C. Goodwin; pages 10, 54, 65, 135, 153, Salmagundi.

CONTENTS

INTRODUCTION

William Sloane Coffin, Jr.

More than seven hundred people spent December 4–5, 1978, at the Riverside Church in New York City learning about the moral, economic, foreign policy, strategic, and theological aspects of the arms race.

The arms race is not a new issue, but it has become the most crucial issue of our time. The terrifying proliferation of modern weaponry makes nuclear cataclysm almost inevitable. Even if we avoid holocaust, the heavy infusion of government funds into the defense budget and away from human needs is killing our society slowly and painfully, day by day.

We see the effects of the arms race everywhere—in rotting, rat-infested housing, outmoded public transportation, inadequate programs of health care and education, rampant unemployment, soaring inflation, and the wrong concept of national security.

As a large institution in an urban setting where these problems are particularly evident, Riverside Church has decided to take the initiative in saying to citizens everywhere: The responsibility is ours; the time is now; and our only hope for any worthwhile future is to REVERSE THE ARMS RACE.

The purpose of our December convocation was educational, because we must know facts in order to communicate our concern to others. That is the only way we shall ever reach our final goal—to

WILLIAM SLOANE COFFIN, JR., is Senior Minister, the Riverside Church.

organize this country so that it becomes politically feasible to think about reversing the arms race. Therefore, we tried to reach those already committed, as well as the uncommitted.

Now let me offer a word to the uncommitted. Some of what you are about to read is pretty strong, because many of us have strong feelings on this subject. If you disagree with the positions in this book, do not let it bother you. It is like going to church when you are a nonbeliever—you just take what you can. Pick out something from a prayer or a nice line from a hymn—whatever you can absorb. Commit as much of yourself to as much of God as you can—that is what Alcoholics Anonymous says. I urge that you take that same line in reading this book. After you go through the convocation addresses, commit as much of yourself to reversing the arms race as your beliefs will allow.

Concerns of the Church

I have no apologies for this conference having been held in a church. In this world, we cannot tolerate the intolerable. Jesus never did, so why should we? But like Jesus, we have to hate evil because we so love the good. If you hate evil more than you love the good, you end up a damn good hater, and that is not our idea. We do not want to tolerate the intolerable. We want to hate what we think is evil, but we want to do it out of such love for the good that the evil becomes

The overflow audience gathered on the floor. Conferees came from forty-two states and the majority had never attended a meeting on disarmament before.

intolerable. This is not anti-American, nor is it against individuals who work in the Pentagon or the White House, but we must name names and be as honest and straightforward as possible.

It was also fitting that this conference be held during the Advent season. In that first Advent, it was very clear to everyone—including Herod—that the Messiah was coming to the poor, and the rich were properly nervous. But in our country, it is blithely assumed that Jesus belongs to the rich, and some of the poor have begun to wonder where their Friend went. Therefore, our concern for the poor—who have become modern-day lepers in this country, while we spend billions upon billions on armaments—is a legitimate concern of the church.

Beyond that, in the first Advent, it was generally assumed that the Messiah was going to be the Prince of Peace. He was going to signal "peace on earth" and not through preparation for war. Now it is blithely assumed that our Savior comes, champagne bottle in hand, ready to break it over the latest nuclear aircraft carrier proposed by the Pentagon.

We have to ask ourselves, "What has happened that everything is upside down?" The clay seems to be saying to the potter, "I made you." The thing made seems to be saying to the maker, "You don't understand; you're naive."

Advent is the season in which we wait for our coming Savior. But we cannot pray for peace and pay for war. To do so is not taking our prayers seriously. We cannot pray, "Thy kingdom come," and then bar its way. We cannot say, "We welcome the Prince of Peace," and gladly empty our pocketbooks for the biggest ballistic binge the world has ever known.

Our Own Kool-Aid Drill

When I consider last November's terrible events in Guyana, I keep returning to one question: At two o'clock in the morning when they were going through the Kool-Aid drill for simultaneous suicide, didn't someone understand the possibility of what might really happen? Suppose someone had said, "This is crazy. We don't want to commit mass suicide. I refuse to drill." That at least would have had the virtue of bringing home some reality.

I suppose most of them took the drill feeling that it could not happen. Perhaps it seemed a little much, but "Well, in life, you know, you have to take the bad with the good. . . . Besides, Rev. Jones is a real dad for us, providing a lot of security. . . . He knows best. . . . He is providing direction for our lives."

Today the Pentagon is the Reverend Jones! Once an honorable

The children "beat the sword into plowshares" by hitting a piñata built to resemble a bomb. It opened to reveal what could be bought in housing, education, etc., for the same funds.

institution, it is showing signs of the same paranoia and megalomania which afflicted Jones in his last months. And like Jones, it has conditioned us—in our case, by ever-rising military budgets which go unopposed—so that we are in the same danger as Rev. Jones's followers, of having passively given over to the Pentagon the power to cause our own destruction. Carter's proposed civil defense drill is like the Kool-Aid drill without the cyanide—preparation for mass suicide of unbelievable dimensions. What will happen to the millions who do not get out of New York City? Of course, the drill is supposed to test our patriotic loyalty and prove our toughness and willingness to die for our country.

But isn't it time for some people to refuse the drill? Isn't it time for somebody to get up and say, "You know this is crazy. . . . This is madness. . . . We are not going into mass exchanges of nuclear weapons." And who should refuse to drink from the giant vats of the Pentagon, if not those who take the cup of salvation from their Lord and Savior? Those who are made strong by the blood of Christ really should have nothing but contempt for the poison processed by the Pentagon. My own strong feeling is that we adopt the spirit of Advent at all times and say, "We refuse it. . . . In the name of the Prince of Peace, we refuse to drill anymore."

Let us now go forth with hearts full of love and divine discontent, and heads full of facts, as we work to Reverse the Arms Race.

William Sloane Coffin, Jr.
June, 1979

HISTORY OF THE ARMS RACE, 1945–1978

Richard J. Barnet

One of the hazards of following Bill Coffin is that any important insight one can come up with, he has come up with first. I confess that the analogy of Reverend Jones and the system of nuclear terrorism that we are operating under struck me too. Such analogies are important because they somehow bring what is such a vast and almost hopelessly enormous subject down to the scale of "ordinary" catastrophe and even tragedy. We can understand nine hundred people, but we cannot understand 140 million—the number that the National Security Council, in its recent publication PRM-10, says will die in a nuclear war.

The Jonestown catastrophe gives a taste of the horror of nuclear terrorism because, as Bill pointed out, it was a drill for death. We are all involved, in one way or another, in that continuing drill for death, not just those concerned with civil defense, but the people who go to the office every day to make plans for the development, production, and use in war of nuclear weapons. They are part of the drill. The people who are involved in war-production and nuclear-trigger factories in places like Rocky Flats are part of the same drill, the psychological and spiritual effects of which we are only now beginning to understand.

RICHARD J. BARNET is co-founder, Institute for Policy Studies, Washington, D. C., a former Kennedy White House staff member, and author of *Global Reach* and *Roots of War*.

Our System of Security

The other aspect of Jonestown which struck me almost the instant I heard about it was the ability of one man, by virtue of a set of beliefs, to bring about the deaths of hundreds of people. We have developed a system of so-called security in which the decision of a leader to sacrifice millions of people is the basis of our state and our society. The power of a leader to sacrifice the people is the essence of nuclear terrorism.

It is now fashionable to worry that a small country, or the Mafia, or just a few individuals anywhere could get hold of a nuclear weapon and threaten society at large with nuclear blackmail. This is a very real, serious, and growing danger, because there is no secret to nuclear weapons. A Princeton undergraduate with no special knowledge of physics was able to develop a plan for putting together a crude bomb on the basis of materials available at the local hardware store. That kind of terrorism is a problem. But I suggest that nuclear terrorism on a larger scale is even more of a problem.

Every American is a hostage and a target and so is every Russian. The 140 million Americans and the more than 100 million Russians who would die in a nuclear war have no control whatever over the decisions of their leaders. They are in the same position as the people of Jonestown. The Russian people cannot control the decision of the Soviet Union to go to Africa, Cuba, or anywhere else, nor can the people of the United States decide whether the president, in his office, will push the button that will bring us nuclear war.

When a man with a gun threatens to shoot the passengers on an airplane unless the president releases some prisoners or pays a ransom, we call that terrorism. But when national leaders threaten millions of deaths—and every nuclear weapon targeted on an enemy city is a direct threat—we call that strategy. That is the fundamental intellectual and moral problem of the nuclear war system and the arms race.

We are at the threshold of a new stage of that arms race—what I would call the third arms race of the postwar period. It is characterized by decisions now being formalized, under which the United States will spend $1.8 trillion in the next ten years. I am sure you have as much difficulty as I do understanding what $1.8 trillion is. Let me just say that it is roughly the same amount that we have spent on arms in the United States from 1945 to the present.

This new stage of the arms race is going to involve a whole series of new weapons systems, including mobile missiles to be based on land, replacing the vulnerable land-based missiles which we have now. We spend a great deal of time and money worrying about the survivability of missiles, but we spend very little time thinking about the survival and survivability of people and societies.

In this new arms race, we will also have a new submarine, the improved Trident, a system that will give a submarine commander the power at his fingertips to destroy four hundred or more population centers in the Soviet Union. But before getting into the real implications of this arms race that we are about to enter, let us go back and see how this all started.

The First Arms Race

The United States first developed nuclear weapons in 1945 for the purpose of winning the war against Japan. We did not have any theory of deterrence. In fact, we had very little theory about it at all. The atomic bomb, as President Truman said, was just another piece of artillery, and to his dying day he contended that nothing much had changed: Weapons had only gotten bigger, not different.

As the arms race began to develop, the United States was always first with the latest technology. We were the first to develop the atomic bomb, the long-range bomber, a deliverable hydrogen bomb—although the Soviets exploded theirs first—the first to have an ICBM, a new hydra-headed multiple-warhead missile (MIRV), the Cruise missile, and so forth. At every stage during this first arms race, the Soviet Union, usually some five years later, duplicated the technological achievements on which the United States had hoped to base its security.

I would agree with Jerome Wiesner, who was President Kennedy's science advisor and is now president of MIT, that this arms race, lasting from 1945 to 1962, was a race that we were running with ourselves. We know now beyond doubt that the Soviet Union was not in the same race. It had neither the capability, nor the funds, nor the national organization after suffering the catastrophic damage of World War II in which twenty million Soviet citizens were killed, to match the United States bomb for bomb or dollar for ruble. The situation was rather asymmetrical. The United States was building a military force which every president said had to be "second to none," and the Soviet Union was developing the same technology very slowly, not attempting to match the United States but rather trying to substitute public relations and bluff for the expenditure of money and the amassing of a huge arsenal.

This was the era of Nikita Khrushchev, who every few years would come out with a pungent statement about Soviet weapons. Their missiles, he said, would hit a fly in outer space. He was producing missiles like sausages—although it turned out that in those days they weren't producing any sausages—but we didn't get the point. However, we got the point they wanted us to get, thanks in large part to the best public relations firm that money could buy—the Department of Defense—whose interest was the same as Khrushchev's, namely, to let everybody think that the Soviets had a big army and a big missile system because that would scare away an attack. The Defense Department also wanted to paint an exaggerated picture of Soviet strength to justify bigger military budgets—and they still do! Neither the Soviet Union nor the United States was really planning to attack the other.

There was deterrence on both sides, but they were deterring different things. The United States, with its huge nuclear arsenal—which today has reached a level of thirty thousand weapons—was trying to deter Soviet political operations. We wanted to make them cautious about exploiting the vulnerable political situation in Western Europe, which many people in the United States government feared would bring Communist governments to power, because in 1947 there were already Communists in the cabinets of Italy and France. So initially, the whole nuclear weapons theory involved developing a power that would keep the Soviet Union from challenging the United States in areas of the world where we did not want that to happen—which was virtually everywhere.

The Soviet Union, on the other hand, was trying to deter an attack on the Soviet Union. From their point of view, the situation in 1948 was extremely dangerous. The United States had a monopoly of nuclear weapons; there was a cold war and a high level of public fear, even hysteria, in the United States. There were many signs of that fear and a total obsession with the Soviet Union. There was an entire issue of *Collier's Weekly* magazine in 1949 devoted to the coming war and defeat of the Soviet Union. It described in detail how the United States would bomb the Soviet Union, occupy it, and then reeducate the people in the religion of free enterprise. And if that was not scary enough, we had a Secretary of the Navy and some generals who made statements during this same period about the necessity, inevitability, and even legitimacy of fighting a so-called "preventative" war. Since the Soviet Union was always paranoid about its security, after wave upon wave of foreign invasions over the centuries, the leaders were frightened and determined to produce the bomb themselves. Every scientist who worked on the atomic bomb testified year after year that an arms race with the Soviet Union was inevitable. There was no doubt that they were going to match us in weapons development.

In the first arms race, the United States had to prove that our nuclear arsenal was credible. It was not only important that we had the weapons, but we also had to demonstrate the will to use them. Many people in this country labor under the illusion that these weapons are not meant to be used. The fact is that people go to work every day, operating on precisely the opposite assumption. And indeed there have been several incidents, particularly in this first arms race, when the possible use of nuclear weapons was considered at an extremely high level of command.

Nuclear War as Strategy

In 1954, according to French Foreign Minister Georges Bidault, Secretary of State John Foster Dulles offered to drop one or more atomic bombs on Communist Chinese territory near the Indo-China border and two atomic bombs against the Vietminh at Dien Bien Phu. Such a historical reminder ought to make us realize how absurd this nuclear arms race is. The Chinese Communists, whom we were seriously considering destroying with a nuclear strike, are now close to becoming allies of the United States.

Here is another example: President Eisenhower, looking back to his arrival at the White House in 1953, said, "I let it be known that if there was not going to be an armistice [this was in Korea]. . . we were not going to be bound by the kind of weapons that we would use. . . . I don't mean to say that we'd have used those big things and destroyed cities," Eisenhower added, "but we would have used enough to win, and we of course would have tried to keep them on military, not civil targets." [1]

Here is a third example: In October, 1962, at the time of the Cuban Missile Crisis, the United States initiated a blockade of Cuba and prepared for an invasion, knowing that there were substantial risks of nuclear war. "We all agreed in the end," Robert Kennedy said afterward, "that if the Russians were willing to go to nuclear war over Cuba, it meant that they were ready to go to nuclear war, and that was that; so they might as well have the showdown then, instead of six months later." And that, I suggest, is exactly how a nuclear war can come about. In my view, the only time a leader will deliberately initiate a nuclear war is when the situation, in his mind, is "nuclear war now or later—better now."

One member of the Joint Chiefs of Staff, Kennedy recalled, felt

[1] Sidney Lens, *The Day Before Doomsday* (New York: Doubleday & Co., Inc., 1977), p. 119.

that we could use nuclear weapons because our adversaries would use theirs against us in an attack. And in 1961, the Kennedy administration seriously contemplated the use of nuclear weapons during the Berlin crisis in which U.S. and Soviet tanks faced each other in the center of the city. Presidential Assistant Arthur Schlesinger, Jr., wrote later:

> While everyone agreed that a Soviet blockade of West Berlin would have to be countered first by a western thrust along the *Autobahn,* there was disagreement between those, like General Norstad [Supreme Commander of NATO at that time], who wanted the probe in order to create a situation where the west could use nuclear weapons and those, like Kennedy and McNamara, who wanted the probe in order to postpone that situation. And, while everyone agreed that we might eventually have to go on to nuclear war, there was disagreement between those who favored a single definitive salvo against the Soviet Union and those who favored careful and discriminate attack.[2]

Even earlier, Douglas MacArthur had proposed using nuclear weapons in Korea. And in 1968, as General William Westmoreland writes in his memoirs, he convened a small secret group in Saigon to study the nuclear defense of Khe Sanh, where the Marine base was in imminent danger of being overrun. Even now, he still thinks that using a few small, tactical nuclear weapons in Vietnam—or even threatening to use them—might have brought the war to an earlier end.

The Second Arms Race

The first arms race ended with the Cuban missile crisis. The Russians found that the policy of bluff did not work, so Khrushchev the money-saver was thrown out, and there began the armament buildup which continues to this day. The Soviet Union has been steadily building in areas of intercontinental missiles and in the development of its forces in Central Europe. It has matched, or perhaps in a purely military sense, even exceeded the United States in certain areas. But the major point is that the military buildup on both sides has been so great that the difference between the thirty thousand nuclear weapons that the United States has and the roughly fifteen thousand that the Soviet Union has is meaningless.

More important are the Soviet submarines off the coast of the United States, carrying about two hundred nuclear weapons, each targeted on an American city and each capable of destroying an American city. The fact that the United States has submarines off the

---

[2] Arthur M. Schlesinger, Jr., *A Thousand Days, John F. Kennedy in the White House* (Boston: Houghton Mifflin Company, 1965), p. 852.

coast of the Soviet Union with three thousand nuclear weapons does not make us one bit safer. The numbers already developed have reached the point where the numbers game is an activity for fools and spendthrifts, not for people who are really interested in saving society or in security for themselves and their families.

The second arms race started with the Soviet buildup which launched the negotiations that we call SALT (Strategic Arms Limitation Talks). For many years, as we all know, there have been negotiations for the purpose of limiting future arms buildups. But during the years of SALT, not one single weapon has been destroyed, and in fact, stockpiles on both sides have doubled and new weapons have been developed.

Today's Arms Race

Most importantly, these have been the years of the major technological developments which have caused the situation I mentioned at the outset and which make the world that we have come through look like a Quaker village in comparison. This third arms race is not just a race of numbers—we have had enough of those numbers to see that they hardly matter. The difference today is in the nature of the technology and of the military doctrine supporting and justifying that technology.

We have both sides—and again the United States is ahead in terms of time and energy—pushing toward highly accurate systems, which means an extremely dangerous situation. These highly accurate warheads, sensitive gear for fighting computer-programmed limited nuclear wars, new and more powerful intercontinental missiles, lasers, killer satellites, and other so-called "war-winning technology" make the military environment far less stable today than it has ever been.

Military planners on both sides are under increasing pressures to keep their forces at a high state of alertness, and simply to resolve the "doubts" that come up all the time—flocks of geese on the radar screen, computer mistakes and breakdowns. All the things that happen in department store billing departments can happen, of course, in military systems, too. With all these human and mechanical errors that are possible, the temptation would be in favor of launching the missiles. We are living in a world where missiles are being programmed to hit missiles; so the premium on going first is enormous. These pressures are making the world a much more dangerous place than it has been at any time since the dawn of the nuclear era.

Potential for Nuclear War

Besides these technological developments, for the first time, nuclear weapons are being drawn into life-and-death political struggles. Wars do not happen "out of the blue." They happen because people feel very strongly and very passionately about political issues. The U.S.-Soviet conflict was not like this. In a way, it was a fight about everything and nothing—but not about anything worthwhile enough to make the leaders on either side push the button that would risk their society.

However, that is not the situation in South Africa for example. The rulers of South Africa, sworn to maintain the domination of nineteen million blacks by four million whites, are obvious customers for the technology of nuclear mass terror. Whether they actually have the bomb or, more likely, are in a position to acquire it rapidly, the threat of a nuclear Masada in Southern Africa is staring us in the face.

Another continuing problem is Iran, with its internal struggles and a huge arsenal of high technology weapons from the United States— all on the border of the Soviet Union.

One can go on and on. The list of potential flash points for nuclear war is a long one; Idi Amin or some other despot with a ravished brain, terrorist groups—it is all possible. The fact is that the world of the first and second arms races was a world that the United States controlled to an extraordinary degree. During much of that period, we had a monopoly or near monopoly of nuclear weapons, and we were the overwhelming economic power in the world. The dollar was better than gold in those days, which is not true today. Now the whole political situation of the world is far more unstable and dangerous.

Therefore, we have to rethink that easy assumption many of us make—I think mostly at a subconscious level—that since we got through one generation of a nuclear arms race, there is no reason why we cannot get through the next. That is why so many nuclear physicists and others who have been working on bombs and military weapons over the years no longer laugh at meetings like this, and in fact, come to these meetings themselves and speak out. They are scared. They are scared for themselves and for their children.

They know that we are mired in a hopeless security strategy. We will spend $1.8 trillion, and the Russians will spend their equivalent of $1.8 trillion. We will increase the military budget 3 percent a year over inflation—an absolutely incredible decision by President Carter, at the very moment when he said he was going to cut and slash to the bone. Cuts are coming from those so-called "frills" which have nothing to do with security—things such as education, child care, health, libraries, police, and fire prevention—so that we can make more bombs. Our use of language is schizophrenic. We reserve the word "strength" for some product of the Department of Defense, but we do not even think about that word as we allow our society to decay. We do not think about the fundamental weakness that comes when a society begins to lose faith in itself.

War by Miscalculation

In the final analysis, the fight between the doves and hawks has very little to do with technology or numbers of weapons. It is important to know about weapons systems, and not very hard, although the subject is one of the most mythicized in the world. Almost any other issue of modern-day living—whether it is figuring out how to get water to our cities, energy, housing, transportation— has far more intellectual content. And these involve much more difficult problems than the subject of the arms race, as far as talking about what to do. But that is not the issue. What really is at stake here is a fundamental disagreement about human nature.

Our whole nuclear weapons system is based on a view of the Russian leaders sitting by a computer, calculating each day how many weapons *we* have, how many weapons *they* have, what the winds will look like on the day of the nuclear war, what the effects will be on the water and transportation systems, how many people will die from radiation. Then some day, the computer will show a magic number of "acceptable casualties"—it may be ten million, twenty million, or fifty million, depending on how evil and sick we think they are. But on that day, they will decide that running a world with the United States out of the way is worth launching a nuclear war. Unless you believe that fantasy of how human beings behave in general, and how these particular Russian leaders are likely to behave in particular, the whole theory behind the amassing of nuclear weapons, the whole justification for building a single additional weapon—or for not destroying half or more of what we have—fades away.

It is not a plausible scenario for nuclear war, but by believing the fantasy and by acting it, we make other scenarios far more plausible. War by miscalculation—this happens when one side or the other says, "It's now or never; we are on an inevitable collision course." The issue becomes, not war or peace, but war *now* or war *then*. That is when one side or the other makes the major miscalculation. Every war is a war of miscalculation. In the First World War, if you have read Barbara Tuchman's account, one side made a move expecting the other side to back down, and the other side did not. The Russians

Founder of the Institute for Policy Studies and a former Disarmament Agency staffer, Richard Barnet addresses the opening session on the history of the arms race.

have done a lot of backing down in major confrontations, but there is no reason to believe that they will always do so in the future.

At the dawn of the nuclear age, Albert Einstein, who not only developed the theory that made the bomb possible, but also wrote the letter launching its production in the United States, said, "Everything is changed except our way of thinking." We have the same habits of mind today in thinking about security and defense that we have had all through history, from the days of bows and arrows to tanks and armies. But times have changed, and if we are going to survive, we must learn that our real strength is not in these useless and dangerous missiles that sooner or later will surely kill us.

Our strength lies in the people who can create, not destroy, who can be proud and free, and who are working to find a way to make a world that they really can leave to their children. This generation has, quite humbly, the final responsibility and the last chance to turn terror into hope.

Questions and Answers

1. Q: DO WE HAVE A POLICY OF "FIRST STRIKE," OVERTLY OR COVERTLY?

A: The United States has an overt policy of reserving the option to use nuclear weapons first. We have consistently refused to sign a "no first use" agreement which, in my view, is a terrible mistake. It is a holdover from the days when we thought the threat to use nuclear weapons was enough to bring about desirable political results in various parts of the world. But it has become clear that in the final analysis, you cannot do that—quite apart from morality—and it is an outrage to think that a nation would risk nuclear war for any of the things that I discussed earlier.

However, President Carter said at the United Nations: "We will not use nuclear weapons first against a country that doesn't have nuclear weapons." But he made it very clear that we *will* use nuclear weapons in Europe and in Korea, and we reserve the right to use them or to threaten their use if necessary to serve what we regard as our interest. What this does is encourage proliferation of nuclear weapons, because it communicates to every country—small as well as large—that even the biggest and most powerful country in the world does not feel secure unless it can use nuclear weapons as ordinary weapons. What is so disturbing about the neutron bomb and some of the other new technology is that it reinforces the notion that these are weapons to be used in specific battlefield situations. The neutron bomb is particularly disturbing because it is a weapon which, by its nature, would be used at very low levels of command. It means putting into the hands of a major, or perhaps someone of lower rank, the decision to initiate the use of nuclear weapons under a battlefield situation.

2. Q: WILL PEOPLE DISARM UNLESS THEY ARE FORCED TO DO SO?

A: We now have a real chance to arrest the arms race, not because people have gotten better, but because the reality of the situation is coming home to more people, and two factors have caused this. For one thing, it has gotten to the point where even winning a war no longer serves a nation's interest. Consider the Second World War— before the proliferation of nuclear weapons—where Germany and Japan were doing rather better than a lot of the so-called victors. In fact, her victories in World War I and World War II ruined Great Britain. I think that the changed nature of war is one reality which, if recognized, will compel people to redefine what national security, or even power, means in the world.

Secondly, there is the economic factor. Until recently, we always assumed in the United States that not only was there no choice between guns and butter, but also that more guns actually made more butter. We may even have believed that the butter depended on the guns. Now I think we are beginning to see, in our cities across the country, that we cannot, as so many presidents used to say, have a military force "second to none" and still do everything we need to do at home. That was the political formula over the last thirty years, but we know it is not true today.

3. **Q:** HOW DO YOU PRESSURE THE PRESIDENT NOT TO MAKE THE NEUTRON BOMB AND OTHER KINDS OF WEAPONS?

A: I think that our weapons policy would change very quickly if the concern which exists in this country was expressed in an organized and political way. The situation now in Washington is not like it was when I was there. At that time, there was a kind of devotion to the military-industrial complex inside the government. If you did not share it, you had no allies, but I think there are allies in the government today. Unfortunately, they feel that the sentiment in this country is overwhelmingly pro-military, mindlessly anti-Soviet, and ready to support any kind of military expenditure that is put forward. What is needed is evidence of a new level of political understanding and consciousness, which can be reflected in traditional letter-writing campaigns or in more sophisticated efforts, such as local communities holding public hearings and inviting their congressional representatives to explain how they plan to vote on the military budget.

To change the climate in this country, we have to begin at the local level—city councils, for example. I think that city councils should discuss the relationship of the defense budget and the proportionate share of the citizens in that city to the budget as a whole and begin to focus public attention on choices. Do we get the MX at "x" billion dollars even if it means giving up this many jobs, this many libraries, police, child-care programs, etc.? Once this happens, I believe that the Pentagon will be in a very weak position with respect to its products, because both defense and deterrence programs are really nonsellers if there is consumer resistance.

4. Q: HOW CAN YOU COUNTER THE FACT THAT SO MANY PEOPLE ARE UTTERLY DEPENDENT ON THE MILITARY FOR THEIR JOBS?

A: There is only one way to counter that, and it involves a serious conversion program in the United States. We can do it. We know how. There are many urgent national needs that would create far more jobs. Putting money into the military is the worst way to spend a billion dollars in order to create jobs. You can spend the same amount in almost any other way and create more jobs. But you have to do the planning; you cannot just let people whose jobs end on Friday afternoon fend for themselves on Monday morning.

What I have proposed is that the president, while waiting for a conversion bill to go through Congress—and there are several good bills in there now—set up, in the White House, a high-level commission on conversion with branches and representatives in every community that is seriously affected by military production. We should make it very clear that the costs of moving toward a real security system are not going to be borne by the people who happen to have been caught in the military-production system. They should not be the ones to pay the price.

I cannot think of anything better than a serious conversion effort to convince the Russian people and others in the world that at last the United States is really serious about reversing the arms race.

LABOR, UNEMPLOYMENT, AND ARMS

Richard Greenwood

One of the things we find in talking about economic conversion is that everyone has his or her own idea of it. Some people wonder if we are talking about economics or religion. Actually, the kind of economics coming out of the White House today probably *is* a religion.

We define "conversion" as job creation in,the civilian sector of the economy for peaceful and socially useful purposes. One of the goals of economic conversion is, first and foremost, to end the arms race. We want to stop the madness—or whatever we are calling it these days—of nuclear deterrence. We want to achieve a state of zero nuclear weapons, as the "Mobilization for Survival" says. A second goal of economic conversion is to achieve a full-employment economy; the third is to halt inflation; and the fourth is to solve the moral dilemma faced by American defense workers.

The Real Cost of the Arms Race

As we look at the arms race today, we must first define the scope of the problem. Here are some equivalencies which may help put the cost of the arms race into perspective:

1. The world's military budget is equal to the annual income of 1.8 billion people in the thirty-six poorest nations;

RICHARD GREENWOOD is Special Assistant to William Winpisinger, International Association of Machinists and Aerospace Workers. He is a former Congressional staff member.

2. In just two days, the world spends on arms the equivalent of a year's budget for the United Nations and all of its specialized agencies;

3. The developed nations spend twenty times more for military assistance than for economic assistance to poorer countries, although the developing nations themselves import arms at the rate of more than $6 billion a year;

4. The United States and the Soviet Union together account for 60 percent of the world's military expenditures, and for 75 percent of the world's arms trade. They have more military forces than all other nations combined;

5. Although first in military strength, these two superpowers rank lower than many other nations in indicators of social well-being, such as infant and maternal mortality rates;

6. World military expenditures average $14,018 per soldier, but public expenditures for education amount to only $230 per school-age child. The cost of one Trident Submarine equals the cost of a year's schooling for sixteen million children in developing countries;

7. The $80 billion spent on arms procurement makes munitions the world's largest industry;

8. Military and space research together get more public research funds than all social needs combined;

9. The cost of the existing stockpile of weapons in the world is estimated at more than twice the value of the capital stock of all manufacturing industry in the United States.

And now there is a new dimension—nuclear power plants. We have only to look at India, which built a nuclear plant with the help of Canada and for seven years was able to work on its first nuclear bomb without being detected. This can happen any time a nuclear power plant goes to Brazil or to any other country that wants to become a nuclear nation. The nuclear fuel for a power plant can be developed into weapons-grade fuel.

The United States alone has put $2 trillion into the military since World War II, and if you want to put $2 trillion into perspective, look at it this way: A person earning $10,000 per year would have to work one billion years to make $1 trillion. What we are saying is that economic conversion would permit transfer of these tremendous, "mind-blowing" resources to the cause of people and peace, rather than power and destruction.

The Cause of Inflation

We can achieve a full-employment economy if we have a national commitment to full employment. Right now, double standards prevail. We are a nation committed to the work ethic, but our official government policy requires the Phillips-Curve tradeoff of full employment for price stability, and it does not work. We have tried it for seven years, and it just does not work. We have had chronically high unemployment, but we have also had double-digit inflation.

Historically, the United States has enjoyed price stability only during periods of relatively full employment, which brings me to the president's Anti-Inflation Program. Among other things, it calls for cutting domestic spending on social programs by $20 billion a year, but it calls for defense spending to grow at a real annual rate of 3 percent. The inflation is in the defense sector of the economy; yet the defense budget is not part of the president's Anti-Inflation Program. We can look at the economy and isolate four other areas of persistent double-digit inflation, and these are the basic necessities of life: energy, food, housing, and health care. But when you look at the president's Anti-Inflation Program, those items are not there either.

Energy is excluded. In fact, we just had a natural gas deregulation bill which is going to mean increases of 20–30 percent for every consumer in the country using natural gas for fuel, heating, and cooking; and if a 20–30 percent increase in the price of fuel isn't inflationary, then I don't know what is. Gasoline is also exempt, along with other kinds of energy.

Raw materials and agricultural products across-the-board are excluded, which includes food. Interest rates are excluded. That means mortgage rates in the housing sector are not brought under so-called restraints, curbs, or voluntary guidelines. In health care, the president proposes to reduce hospital costs by 2 percent a year, but that is going to require legislation from a conservative to reactionary Congress. Besides that, the proposal does nothing to restructure the health care industry, which is really the only way we will ever get a handle on health care costs.

Every employer in this country will enforce the wage guidelines with glee, but there is nobody on the Council for Wage-Price Stability who will ever police the prices of the corporations—defense contractors in particular. What will happen is a very simple exercise in juggling the books in order to get the most—the profit maximization theory. Defense contractors may lower some prices in the civilian sector, but they will use "cost-plus" contracting methods and noncompetitive bidding to make up for whatever they may save on the civilian side, and their profit levels will not be harmed one bit.

The Defense Industry

It is ironic that the closest thing to a nationalized industry in this country is the defense industry. When the job runs out, the weapons system becomes obsolete, or the contract expires or is terminated, then the defense industry throws its workers onto the open market and calls it free enterprise. But the corporate contractor, as in the case of the Rockwell Corporation with the B-1 bomber, receives indemnity payments for the loss of profits it would have made, had the contract continued or follow-ons occurred. What this means is that, particularly in the defense industry, we have socialism for the corporation and free enterprise for the workers. And as long as the defense planners' imperative remains that of technological superiority, then productive plant capacity and manpower will remain as redundant input into that system.

As a matter of fact, 60 percent of the defense capacity is idle right now. Technology will ceaselessly replace human workers in defense production, especially with the advent of energy-directed weapons. This increases the possibility of total push-button warfare and all that might follow. As long as defense contractors are permitted unbridled profit-maximization prerogatives, with no accountability to society, to the workers, or to the communities in which plants are located, then they will continue to sell defense technology anywhere in the world—the way a record-breaking $13 billion in weaponry was sold around the world by U.S. manufacturers last year. And that was after President Carter's pious commitment to curb the arms traffic and rein in the merchants of death.

As this technology is scattered, U.S. workers not only lose jobs, but every nation's security is threatened, and the risk of war increases tremendously. In passing, as we look at the proliferation of both nuclear and conventional weapons, we need to review the pages of history and ask ourselves: Who knows where we may find the megalomania of the world's next Hitler? In Uganda? In Brazil? In Argentina? In Chile? In Nicaragua?

Job Blackmail

Economic conversion, then, is in our self-interest. This is how a machinist will feel. Economic conversion will help solve the moral dilemma faced by American defense workers. International President Bill Winpisinger calls this moral dilemma "job blackmail," and it works like this. Each time a new weapons system comes up for a vote in Congress, or a military base is threatened with closure, or an obsolete weapons contract expires, then an outcry begins: "We need the system. . . . We need weapons for jobs. . . . We need to save the base. . . . Save the system to save our jobs, our business and our communities."

Most of us fervently hope for peace and an end to the arms race, but in this society and this system, one cannot survive without a job and an income. Our employers know this even better than the rest of us, and they have been using it for years to whip us into line. Driven by the quest for profits, they come to the trade unions and they say, "Together let us go to Congress and the Pentagon and save our jobs." It happened with Lockheed three years ago and the Machinists helped bail them out. We are not proud of that. It also happened with the B-1 and more recently in the sale of jets to the Mid-East.

International President Winpisinger testified before the Senate Foreign Relations Committee against the sale of those jets, and during the question period former Senator Griffin of Michigan looked at him and said, "How can you sit there, as President of the Union with more at stake in production of the F-5E and the F-15 and the F-16 than anybody else, and testify against this sale? This means jobs for your members!" Bill Winpisinger looked back at him, and he said, "Senator, no self-respecting machinist wants a damn job at the cost of war."

The Machinists Union is tired of job blackmail. We are tired of being the instrument of an industry that is bloated, wasteful, and on the path of certain holocaust; an industry devoid of moral principles and oblivious to any kind of social accountability. We know who, in the crunch, is going to be called upon to do the dirty work when they have played all their games and everything is in line for the next war. Who is going to do the fighting, the dying, and the sacrificing? It will be the sons and daughters of the working people in this country. Corporate executives will probably be able to arrange things such as college deferments for their sons and daughters. But we, the working people of this country, cannot even afford to send our sons and daughters to college today.

We know who will do the fighting and the dying, and we reject that legacy. We do not want it! We will not stand for it! Economic conversion will solve this dilemma for our country's workers. We know we can get jobs in the civilian sector of the economy, making socially useful and purposeful products for the benefit of all the people, rather than working to the detriment of the economy and the human race.

Economic Conversion

Planned economic conversion means advance notice of defense cutbacks at the local level—notice to the community and to the workers. It means using that early warning system to prepare for the day when the weapons contract expires, when the technology changes or is sold overseas, when production ceases and the plant closes, or when there are cutbacks in employment. Planned economic conversion means drawing up alternatives for military production, using the same plant, the same equipment, the same workers, and the same community. It will have to mean short-term income and benefit guarantees to displaced defense workers, and it will mean training and retraining for some of the workers being relocated. And above all, planned economic conversion means a national commitment to full employment by federal, regional, state, and local planning bodies.

Inside the plant itself, planned economic conversion means setting up alternative-use committees to decide what can be produced: how to beat "swords into plowshares." Given the current climate of labor-management relations, these committees cannot be joint or tripartite. Corporate America has declared war on the trade union movement, and we simply cannot sit at the table with them on these kinds of ventures. In the first place, they do not want us there. They would rather have a union-free environment. So the trade unions will have to set up their own committees, although we would like to have them set up by corporate management. But how do you force corporations when they apparently are not interested? Legislative penalties might be one answer.

The affected community must have some say because we do not want to go from a weapons system to something that may be harmful to the environment or detrimental to society in some other way. The point is that both the workers and the communities must have a role in answering the question: "What do we do now that the defense work has stopped?" And that is a tough question, although not particularly so for corporations, because capital is highly mobile. It can move anywhere it wants to, and it is on the move continually. But labor is not mobile, and communities are not mobile. So what do we do when the defense work stops? We do the things that I have just outlined.

We must also remember this: We know that $1 billion spent anywhere else in the economy will create more jobs than $1 billion spent in defense. Defense production is extremely capital-intensive. Capital and technology are substituted for labor, and the hardware of defense production is consumed only once. It is made to self-destruct. It is not used in the production of other goods and services, which means there is no multiplier principle, or downstream economic activity, or job and income generation. One big bang and it's all over, unless it sits unused in a stockpile or on the shelf of death and destruction.

We will get a healthier bang for a billion dollars in the civilian sector of the economy, and we can always start out with a little catalog to tell us where we find these jobs and these products. For example, solar, wind, and bio-mass alternative energy systems, small-scale hydro manufacturing jobs—plus installation and maintenance—will create many more well-paid, union-scale jobs than we are getting out of defense. The effect will ripple throughout the economy, through retail and other supporting services. What about more jobs modernizing and rehabilitating our railroads? Let us rebuild the physical infrastructures of our older cities—sewers, water systems, streets, bridges, schools, mass transit systems. Economic conversion can also mean rural development opportunities. It could help stop the decline of the family farm and the decline of small rural communities where there is real poverty.

In short, economic conversion must be an important component of any full-employment program in this nation.

NUCLEAR WEAPONS SPENDING

Paul F. Walker

My colleagues and I in the Boston Study Group have been looking at defense spending over the last seventy years. We have been in a period of relative peace—thirty years of peace—if one disregards those "little battles" of Korea and Vietnam. And yet, we are spending more today for defense, even accounting for inflation, than we spent at any other time in the twentieth century, except for World War II. We have surpassed World War I and Korea, and we are at about the same level as we were in Vietnam. It is true that much of the increase is accounted for by inflation and by military and civilian pay raises during the last ten years. But a good part of it is due to the increasingly sophisticated and expensive technology of our weapons systems. Let us look at nuclear weapons first.

The New Nuclear Weapons

We began thirty years ago with a nuclear weapons strategy called "massive retaliation." That evolved into what is called "mutual assured destruction"—the MAD System. Now we are getting away from MAD and into a period of what one might call "nuclear war fighting." I want to try to explain this change by looking at three of the most dangerous and destabilizing of the literally hundreds of innovations we are seeing in nuclear technology.

PAUL F. WALKER is a Fellow, Kennedy School of Government, Harvard University. He is a former Russian intelligence specialist, Army Security Agency, and coauthor of *The Price of Defense: A New Strategy for Military Spending*.

The first major innovation, which began during the last ten years and is continuing at an escalating rate, is an increased number of warheads per weapon. When the United States stopped deploying land-based, sea-based, and air-based weapons in 1967, we had about 1,710 ICBMs and SLBMs. But since then, that number has risen to approximately 12,000 strategic nuclear warheads, and that is during a time of arms control negotiations—we have signed SALT I, and we are working on SALT II. Similarly, the Soviets had 1,000 or so warheads in the early 1970s, and they have 4,000–5,000 warheads now. Clearly, we are seeing an enormous vertical proliferation in nuclear warheads. A limit on the number of weapons has not been effective in limiting the destructive potential of the nuclear forces.

The second major innovation is the increased destructiveness of these strategic weapons. Weapons used on Hiroshima and Nagasaki were in the range of ten to twenty kilotons apiece, and they each killed about one hundred thousand people. Today we are talking about warheads in the range of one hundred kilotons, five hundred kilotons—up to twenty-five megatons. If you consider the area of destructiveness, assuming five pounds per square inch overpressure for certain weapons, there were about three square miles destroyed by the Hiroshima and Nagasaki bombs. With the new weapons being produced and possibly deployed in the future—the MX Missile being one—we are talking about 235 square miles potentially destroyed by each individual weapon. In short, nuclear warheads are proliferating and the destructiveness of each individual weapon is greatly increasing as well.

The third major innovation involves accuracy. We started off in the early sixties with a Titan ICBM that had an accuracy of between one-half mile and a mile. We are now talking about accuracies in the range of 200 to 300 feet, while some of the systems already being deployed probably have accuracies of 200 to 400 yards. In other words, we are talking about a missile coming from Moscow and being able to hit the Riverside Church after a 6,000 mile flight. That is a very high degree of accuracy.

About two years ago, Charles Stark Draper, founder of Draper Laboratories in Cambridge, was discussing inertial guidance systems and ICBM accuracies, and he said, "Given enough time, and given enough money, we can get an accuracy down to one-tenth of an inch over a 6,000 mile flight, at 20,000 miles per hour." That probably involves more advances in mapping techniques than it does in inertial guidance. The use of satellites for photography has made possible much greater accuracy in mapping.

Escalating Costs

Let us look at the individual systems and see some average costs, which are also important. For example, we have something called the B-1 bomber. People think the B-1 bomber is gone, but it is not. We still fund research in strategic bombers, and we are talking about what is called an FB-111 which would be a smaller version of the B-1 bomber. If we actually deploy those systems, we are talking about $100–200 million apiece, maybe more.

We also have what is called the MX Missile, the mobile missile— the multiple-aim-point-system replacements for the land-based missile systems. This system, which has a very good chance of being deployed in some mode, will cost anywhere from $30–50 billion. Then there are the Trident Submarines, at about $2 billion apiece. These have been delayed, but we currently have seven or eight scheduled for completion. And we have other advances in nuclear weapons, such as the anti-satellite systems, enhanced command and control, and ABM systems. These new technologies to replace the present nuclear Triad could total $100 billion or more in this century.

The point I want to make with regard to nuclear systems is that there is a growing emphasis on "offense." Accuracy and destructiveness are increasing and penetration is improving. Regardless of what you read in the *New York Times* about laser- and particle-beam technology, defensive ABM systems do not look very good. I would say that offense is really dominant.

Conventional Weapons

However, on the conventional nonnuclear side, the idea of defense is becoming more dominant. We have also gained a high degree of destructiveness and accuracy in conventional weapons, especially since the mid-1960s. We saw a Styx missile destroy the Elath, an Israeli destroyer, in the 1967 Mid-East War. That was a $20,000 missile that knocked out a $1½ million ship, and we are finding that to be more and more of a possibility. It also happened in Vietnam with laser-guided Hobo and Maverick bombs and TV-guided optical systems. I predict that defense will become more and more dominant in terms of new precision-guided technology in the conventional sphere.

What does this mean for war in general? For a balanced situation such as Central Europe it means that people no longer have much ground to argue that we have to meet the Soviets, tank for tank or artillery piece for artillery piece. If we want to—and that is questionable—we can now deploy accurate systems to defend Western Europe, South Korea, or some other area without being offensively threatening to an opponent. In fact, this might even act as a catalyst for starting to disarm those particular arms-race areas.

Future Defense Strategy

Let me make four concluding points. First, remember that the number of cities in the world is not really growing; it is not expanding. Yet the destructiveness of conventional arsenals, and particularly the nuclear arsenals, is expanding enormously. All we have to do is look at the possibilities for nuclear exchanges between the Soviets and the Americans. A few years ago there were a couple of thousand warheads around, but today, we are talking about twelve thousand strategic warheads and twenty-two thousand tactical warheads in the United States, all of which are larger than the bombs dropped on Hiroshima and Nagasaki. That is a total of about thirty-five thousand warheads for the United States; for the Soviets, we are talking in the range of ten thousand strategic and tactical warheads.

Former Secretary of Defense Robert McNamara estimated back in the 1960s that to maintain a mutual assured destruction system, we needed to be able to destroy, in a second strike, 30 percent of the Soviet population and 70 percent of the industry, all of which is concentrated in about two hundred cities and certain industrial centers—hydroelectric plants and all. In other words, we are talking about the ability to destroy the Soviet Union with two hundred weapons; yet our arsenals contain in the neighborhood of thirty-five thousand weapons. We have to ask ourselves, "Is that really the safe approach?"

Secondly, as I mentioned earlier, we are getting away from a system of mutual assured destruction. President Carter emphasized in a recent press conference that our nuclear strategy is based on mutual deterrence. Yet I would argue that if one looks at the new systems coming about—the higher accuracies, increased yield-to-weight ratios, and the increased numbers—one can only conclude that these are not particularly supportive of a mutual deterrence system. They are supportive of a war-fighting strategy, and I think the Soviets are going the same way. Whether that will make the use of nuclear weapons more likely, I do not know, but that is something we should reflect upon.

Thirdly, let us remember the enormous costs for the new nuclear and conventional systems today. We are talking about $50 billion for a mobile land-based ICBM system, and even in the conventional sphere, about $25 million for a jet fighter. Back in World War II, that same money probably would have bought two squadrons of aircraft. Even the M-60 tank, which cost $300,000 five years ago, today costs $700,000, and the new tank we are talking of deploying, the XM-1, is estimated to cost in the range of $1½million. The cost of weaponry is getting to be prohibitive, and I suggest that we will have either a very large military in the future, heavily armed with very cheap weapons, or a small military, lightly armed with very expensive weapons.

Finally, every system has externalities to it. You can build a Cadillac only so big, and we are finding that the Cadillac is getting smaller. A country can expand only up to a certain point before it starts to antagonize its neighbors and endanger its own foreign policy. The U.S. defense budget is predicted to reach $175 billion three years from now. Compared to the Gross National Product of the rest of the world, the Department of Defense budget is bigger than the budgets of 142 of those 150 countries. In terms of budget, our Pentagon is the eighth largest country in the world. But we are coming to the point where more dollars do not necessarily mean better defense. We are getting to the point where the budget must be limited in some sense.

We have argued that over the next ten years the defense budget could be reduced by as much as 45 percent, slowly and incrementally, continually reassessing American foreign policy. In today's dollars, that would mean a budget of probably $75–80 billion. I would argue that a budget of that size, if it takes new technologies and disarmament seriously, can better defend this country and its worldwide commitments and also act as a catalyst toward arms control and disarmament.

ARMS SALES AND REPRESSION

Michael T. Klare

As if developments in the design of nuclear and conventional weapons were not frightening enough, let us consider the even more frightening diffusion of those weapons throughout the world.

Between 1950 and 1978, the United States sold or gave away approximately $153.5 billion worth of arms, ammunition, and implements of war to the other countries of the world. Since the United States supplies approximately one-half of all the arms traded on the international market, you can double that figure to about $300 billion to get a sense of how many dollars worth of weapons have been transferred internationally in the past twenty-eight years.

Figures of this magnitude are difficult to comprehend. What does $153.5 billion really mean? According to the U.S. Department of Defense, it means that in those years, the United States sold or gave away a total of 17,971 combat aircraft including: 915 F-5s; 3,936 F-84s; and 972 F-4 Phantom fighter-bombers. In addition, it means 4,079 helicopters; 4,044 warships; 21,795 other vessels; 31,950 tanks; 48,640 other armored vehicles; and a total of 263,166 guided missiles—not to mention countless millions of rifles and small arms of all kinds. Enough weapons, in other words, to fight World War II all over again or to fight a much more dangerous and destructive World War III.

MICHAEL T. KLARE is Director of the militarism and disarmament project, Institute for Policy Studies, and author of *War Without End: American Planning for the Next Vietnams* and *The Doomsday Trade* (forthcoming).

The War Business

I have given these precise figures for the number of weapons transferred because I want to make clear that what we are talking about here are the instruments of war. It is very fashionable in Washington to talk about arms as if they were just some other product of U.S. manufacturers being sold for the benefit of mankind. Indeed, it is normal to name weapons after late-model automobiles. For instance, we have the Falcon missile, the Tomcat aircraft, the Matador missile, the Maverick missile, and so on. In addition, there are arms bazaars held all over the U.S. where these things are promoted just as if they were consumer goods. In fact, you can even find representatives of the U.S. government who have the nerve—or the cynicism—to describe weapons as if they were somehow instruments of peace, rather than war. Thus there is the F-5A, of which we have sold 915 to foreign governments, which is known as the Freedom Fighter. And there is another plane, the AU-23 counter-insurgency plane, armed with napalm, which we have sold to the Thais. It is called the Peace-Maker.

I don't think we should be misled or mystified by these descriptions. Sales of weapons can have political purposes. They can also have economic purposes—to balance the budget or to improve the stability of the dollar—and they can have diplomatic purposes, such as making friends and allies. The transfer of weapons can have many different uses, but the weapons themselves can be used for one thing only, and that is to kill people. And make no mistake about it, our government and the other major arms suppliers are selling weapons to governments which are using them, not as symbols of national prestige or to modernize their economy as is often suggested, but to kill people.

American arms are being used at this very moment to slaughter human beings like ourselves in many areas of the world. Thousands have been killed in Nicaragua by American M-16 rifles and bomb-laden C-47 transports sold to the Nicaraguan National Guard. Indonesian forces today are using U.S.-made OV-10 Bronco counter-insurgency planes to bomb the people of East Timor because they are resisting Indonesia's illegal efforts to take over that area. Every day we read reports of dozens of people being killed in places such as the Philippines, Thailand, Argentina, and the Spanish Sahara—all of them victims of American weapons.

Nowhere is the true meaning of U.S. arms sales more evident than in Iran, where thousands of people have died in the past few months for the crime of wanting to live without a king. For years, the Shah was our number-one arms customer, taking about 25 percent of all the arms exported by the U.S. government under the Foreign Military Sales Program. We were told that these weapons were needed primarily to help Iran defend itself against a potential Soviet attack on its northern borders. But the real priorities of U.S. arms sales to Iran were, first, to help the Shah defend himself against his own people, and second, to equip Iran to act as a kind of local police power on behalf of U.S. interests in the Persian Gulf.

To be specific, we have sold Iran F-4 fighter-bombers, which are deep-penetration strike weapons, F-5 counter-insurgency planes, helicopter gunships, and other weapons which have no use whatever in defending Iran against Soviet attack. We also supplied SAVAK, the Secret Police, with small arms, clubs, riot gear, and other instruments of repression. These weapons were used in the streets of Tehran and dozens of other Iranian cities in the attempt to put down the revolt against the Shah.

Arms Production Abroad

Ambitious Third-World leaders, such as the Shah of Iran, many of whom have been trained in the United States, have become convinced that the shortest path to what the press calls "modernization" is to recreate the U.S. military-industrial-space complex in their homelands. Since they lack the technological capabilities and resources to create such a monster, they have hired U.S. companies to come in and build entire arms industries from scratch. Not only are we selling the instruments of war and the instruments of repression to foreign governments, but we are also selling the technology to produce these weapons. Northrop is building an aircraft factory in Taiwan; Colt Industries has built rifle factories in the Philippines and South Korea; Textron has been building a helicopter factory in Iran, and so forth.

Other countries, including Brazil, Argentina, Pakistan, Indonesia, Turkey, and Israel, have become partners of U.S. arms corporations in so-called coproduction projects, whereby they produce U.S. arms under license. To me, these projects are even more dangerous than straight arms sales because they enhance a country's capacity to wage war on a prolonged basis. In fact, some of these countries have gone into the arms market themselves, selling weapons on their own to still other governments in order to pay for all of the high-technology weapons they are importing from the United States.

The result of all this is that diffusion of the means of violence is increasing at an exponential rate. The last thing an undeveloped country needs is a miniaturized version of the U.S. military-industrial complex, with all the waste, corruption, and distorted priorities that we have had to endure in this country with our own military-industrial complex.

Not only are we selling arms and the technology to produce them, but we are also selling the skills of our scientists and engineers to maintain, repair, and operate the weapons and the weapons factories. Since many Third-World countries are demanding modern arms faster than they can produce trained technicians to perform all the functions that arms maintenance and operation require, these regimes have hired tens of thousands of American technicians— many of them former military personnel—to come and perform such functions. In Iran, for instance, thousands of U.S. technicians working with Lockheed, Northrop, and Bell Helicopter were brought in to perform all the back-up work on the hundreds of F-4s, F-5s, F-15s, and AH-1G gunships that we sold to the Shah over the past ten years. Thousands more work in Saudi Arabia, Kuwait, Oman, and Jordan, as well as other Middle East countries. I call these people "white-collar mercenaries" because they wear suits and ties and carry attaché' cases instead of rifles. But they are still mercenaries in the sense that they perform critical functions in other countries' armies. These technicians became so crucial to the Iranian war machine that the Senate Foreign Relations Committee reported in 1976:

> There is a general agreement among U.S. personnel involved with Iranian programs, that it is unlikely that Iran could go to war in the next five to ten years, with its current and prospective inventory of sophisticated weapons . . . without U.S. support on a day-to-day basis.

In other words, the United States has been at war because the Iranian Army has been at war against the people of Iran. I can picture very easily American white-collar mercenaries punching out the orders on their computer consoles—all run by Americans—to send troops from one part of Tehran to another in order to put down student demonstrations.

Perhaps that will explain the anti-American feelings of the Iranian opposition—based on a perception of the United States, because of the white-collar mercenaries, as an instrument of repression and militarism. By the same token, if Saudi Arabia were to go to war with another country, U.S. white-collar mercenaries would be involved in the key military facilities of their army—the radar sets, the communications sets, the intelligence systems, and so forth—and therefore would be among the first casualties in any such war. The obvious conclusion is that the United States itself could very easily be drawn into any such conflict, simply because of the numbers of American casualties that would result from any war involving those countries.

Yet Congress and the press tend to regard the white-collar mercenaries as no different from any other U.S. technicians working abroad. Moreover, neither the white-collar mercenaries nor any of the programs for exporting America's military arms-production capability are covered by Carter's arms sales policy, which means that we are increasing the world's stock of war-making capabilities at a time of growing conflict and instability in many parts of the globe. At the same time, we are increasing the risk that the United States will be drawn into local conflicts abroad. Since other major industrial powers including the U.S.S.R., France, Britain, and West Germany are doing much the same thing, we are laying the foundations for a global conflagration of unprecedented scope and magnitude.

Even U.S. government officials admit that they do not know the consequences of everything they are doing. Recently, Leslie Gelb, head of the Bureau of Politico-Military Affairs in the State Department, testified before Congress:

> When these arms are delivered, and when the recipients learn to use them, they will change the face of world politics. For the first time, many states throughout the world will have arms of much the same sophistication and quality as those of the few major powers.

I hardly need add that the simultaneous proliferation of nuclear war capabilities means that any local conflict could very easily and rapidly escalate into a full-scale thermonuclear conflagration.

When I raise these concerns in Washington, I am told that arms sales have all kinds of benefits for the American public that we have to take into account, such as easing the balance-of-payments problem, helping to buttress the sinking dollar, and providing jobs for American workers. I am also told that we need arms sales in order to guarantee our access to oil, to gain political leverage with countries such as Saudi Arabia, and to cement our alliances with NATO and other friendly countries. There is also the argument that if *we* do not sell arms, somebody else will; and finally, that arms sales are essential to U.S. national security.

Most of these arguments do have some validity. For example, arms sales do help the balance of payments. But I would argue that when the fate of humanity is at stake, no excuse on earth justifies the sale of the instruments of slaughter to the war-makers of the world. I think we therefore have an important responsibility not only to fight against the threat of thermonuclear war involving the superpowers, but also to do whatever we can to stop the further proliferation of arms-making capabilities in other countries of the world.

Folksingers Pete Seeger and Fred Kirkpatrick lead the congregation in singing "Down by the Riverside" during the liturgy.

CONVENTIONAL ARMS SALES

Cindy Arnson

There is an aspect of the conventional arms trade that one hears very little about, especially in these days of an announced commitment to human rights. That is the trade in weapons designed for internal security. This repression gear includes such items as tear gas, riot sticks and shields, armored cars, counter-insurgency planes, pistols, shotguns, and rifles. Although sales of these weapons constitute only a small part of the more than $13 billion in annual U.S. arms sales, they represent one of this country's most direct contributions to oppression abroad. Because of the nature of these items, they are also the most likely to have a direct impact on the people of the Third World.

Arms and Human Rights

For example, in the last five or six years, the United States has sold armored cars to the Palace Guard of Haiti; chemical mace and pepperfog to the National Police in South Korea; and pistols, revolvers, and ammunition to the Imperial Iranian Gendarmerie. And just four months into the Carter Presidency, despite an announced human rights policy, the State Department allowed the delivery of five thousand M-15 rifles to the Nicaraguan National Guard. In fact, during the summer of 1978, Congress finally required

CINDY ARNSON works with the Institute for Policy Studies, Washington, D.C. She is a former researcher for the Center for International Policy.

that such items as thumbscrews, shock batons, and leg irons be licensed before being exported.

But to understand more fully the relationship between arms sales and human rights, it is important to look at some of the reasons for U.S. arms sales overseas.

Immediately after World War II, the vast majority of U.S. arms exports went to the so-called "forward defense" countries on the fringes of the Soviet Union and China. This was the period of "containing Communism," as the United States cemented regional pacts, such as NATO and CENTO, and sought to rebuild free-world armies exhausted by six years of war.

Starting in the late 1950s, and especially after the Cuban Revolution, the United States began to sell arms for an entirely different reason. The emphasis shifted from defense against external aggression to defense against what was called "subversion from within"—the Pentagon's catch phrase for popular movements seeking democratic rights, social justice, or a basic overthrow of the existing order.

Combating guerrillas or just keeping track of dissidents required a whole arsenal of counter-insurgency gear, ranging from light aircraft to armored cars, small arms, and tear gas. Millions of dollars worth of this kind of equipment was transferred to selected Third-World regimes through Military Assistance Program grants and through the Foreign Military Sales Program throughout the 1960s. To understand the link between arms sales of this kind and human rights violations, let us look at Nicaragua.

Arms for Nicaragua

Despite the fact that the United States has not sent in the Marines of late and is trying to direct a negotiated settlement, this country bears a heavy responsibility for the terror and destruction that Somoza's National Guard has unleashed on the Nicaraguan population. After sending troops into Nicaragua twice in the early twentieth century, the U.S. Marines set up the National Guard to keep "stability and order" in the country. When the Sandinista National Liberation Front, which is spearheading the current opposition, was formed in the early 1960s, the United States sent to General Anastasio Somoza enough planes to give him the largest air force in Central America. In the early 1970s, after the Sandinistas stepped up their activities, the U.S. sold additional counter-insurgency planes, transport aircraft, utility helicopters, armored cars, rifles, pistols, and ammunition to Somoza under the Foreign

Military Sales Program. It is no exaggeration to say that virtually every tank, plane, and bullet used by Somoza's forces in the recent fighting was of U.S. origin. Although U.S. officials would prefer to distance themselves now from General Somoza, they cannot deny the history of U.S. involvement. Once we have sold arms, we have very little chance to reproach those who use them, however brutally.

U.S. Arms in Iran

It is the same story in Iran. Besides arming the Shah with the most advanced, sophisticated weapons available, we were also deeply involved in the arming of his internal security forces. Under the Commercial Sales Program conducted through the State Department, private U.S. firms in the past few years sold thousands of revolvers and ammunition to the National Police. To the Imperial Iranian Gendarmerie—the Shah's own "national guard"—the United States sold some fifty thousand grenades and other explosives, and the usual repression array of small arms, communication equipment, and spare parts.

More numbers—under the Foreign Military Sales Program, the Iranian Army purchased 356,000 gas masks and 12,000 tear gas cannisters. And on November 5, 1978, the State Department announced that in addition to tear gas, it was ready to send special United States advisors to Iran to help train the Shah's troops in riot control. All of this is on top of the tanks, jeeps, and helicopters that the U.S. has supplied to the Shah's army for the past twenty-five years. The distinction between arms supplied to keep the Soviet hordes from pouring down from the north and arms supplied for internal repression entirely loses its meaning.

I do not mean to imply that U.S. sales of advanced fighters, naval carriers, precision-guided missiles, and the like are necessarily for use in internal repression. Here the link between arms sales and human rights is much less direct. But if you look at the customers for these advanced weapons—the Shah of Iran, Ferdinand Marcos in the Philippines, the military governments of Thailand and Indonesia, Park in South Korea—you begin to see a very disturbing pattern, for these are the very regimes most often cited for gross violations of human rights, including the use of torture.

Today in the late 1970s, the United States is using arms sales to cement relationships with these so-called "friendly" regimes. Thus, to challenge the arms sales abroad is to do two things: First, it is to question a basic foreign-policy assumption that the interests of the United States coincide with the interests of these dictators. Second, and more important, it is to lend support to people in various parts of the Third World who are struggling against these militaristic regimes whose very policies and priorities are inimical to the guarantee of political, social, and economic rights in their own countries.

Riverside volunteers sold literature.

DEFENSE POLICY OBJECTIVES

Randall Forsberg

Few people in the United States know that most of the military budget goes neither to nuclear weapons nor to Third World arms sales, but to our own conventional forces, which have three parts. First, we have the Army and the Marines, with ground troops that seize and hold land areas and fight with tanks, artillery, and rifles. Second, there are the Air Force's tactical aircraft—fighter and attack planes that give the ground troops close air support, do longer range interdiction bombing behind enemy lines, or fight enemy bombers and fighters in the air to prevent them from doing those things to us. Finally, there is the Navy, excluding their strategic nuclear submarines.

U.S. Conventional Forces

I draw attention to these forces for two reasons. For one thing, they account for about 80 percent of our military budget, whereas offensive strategic nuclear weapons account for only about 20 percent. It is essential to be aware of them and prepare alternatives to them if we are to make substantial cuts in military spending. Secondly, the rationales for these conventional forces are intimately tied to the motivating reasons now being given for continuing the strategic nuclear arms race. If we want to stop the nuclear arms race,

RANDALL FORSBERG is lecturer on military policy and arms control, Massachusetts Institute of Technology, coauthor of *The Price of Defense: A New Strategy for Military Spending* and author of *American Peace Directory*.

we have to understand the linkage between strategic and tactical nuclear weapons on the one hand, and conventional arms on the other. We must devise effective ways to weaken this linkage, or get around it, while still reducing the conventional arms that make up most of this country's defense industry.

Why do we maintain conventional forces in a nuclear age? Why do we have a permanent two-million-man standing army in peacetime, in addition to our 10,000 long-range nuclear warheads? Before World War II, the size of the standing army in the United States was never greater than 200,000. Before World War I, it was never greater than 20,000. With all the talk about national defense and Soviet threats, one might think that the avowed purpose of our troops would be national defense. But that is not the case. Neither the Soviet Union nor any other country has the transport ships and aircraft, the foothold in this hemisphere, or the protected logistics lines that would be required to mount a major conventional assault on this country.

In fact, the only military forces that can threaten the United States directly are the Soviet intercontinental nuclear missiles. Since the Soviet Union built up a large arsenal of these missiles in the late 1960s, paralleling our buildup in the early part of the decade, all major U.S. cities, down to a size of 25,000–50,000 people, have been laid open to the threat of a missile attack. Nothing can protect us from such an attack—not our nuclear forces nor our conventional arms. It is true that we try to prevent nuclear attack by threatening retaliation in kind with our own land- and submarine-based missiles. However, the threat of retaliation is a psychological deterrent *before* the fact. It offers no defense should some leader decide to use nuclear weapons.

Our conventional forces—to answer the original question—have two main functions: One is to help defend Western Europe in the event of a major war there with the Soviet Union; the other is to intervene in Third World conflicts where the Soviet Union is not involved directly, as in the Vietnam War.

Roughly half of our ground forces—the Army's mechanized and armored divisions with tanks and artillery—are well-suited for the European situation, while the other half—the Marines and the Army infantry units with much less heavy equipment—can fly into an area or come over a beach and are more suited to Third-World conflicts. In fact, they would be ill-prepared to face Soviet tank armies in Europe.

Similarly, the Navy can be divided into two major parts. The

Navy's Power Projection Forces include aircraft carriers and amphibious assault ships, in addition to escort ships, embarked aircraft, and supply ships. These large, expensive vessels, which are quite vulnerable to Soviet nuclear attack, take about half of the Navy's nonstrategic budget. They are mainly useful for going to distant parts of the world where we do not have enough popular support to secure land bases and for launching an attack from the sea. The United States is the only country in the world capable of intervening on a large scale—with several hundred thousand men, not merely tens of thousands, as is happening right now in Africa with Cuba and the Soviet Union—in regions of the world not contiguous to its own territory. In that sense, the United States is the world's only global military power.

The other component of the U.S. Navy consists of Sea Control Forces. These are composed of anti-submarine patrol aircraft, submarines, and convoy escorts, whose primary purpose is to keep the North Atlantic sea lanes open for resupply in case there is another long, conventional World-War-II-type conflict in Europe, with the U.S.S.R. replacing Germany as the enemy.

Conventional and Nuclear Arms

What is the connection between these conventional forces and the nuclear arms race? It lies in the possibility of escalation.

All the conventional forces which I have been describing are equipped with high-explosive bombs and shells and with alternative nuclear armaments called tactical nuclear weapons. Our tactical nuclear weapons are even more numerous than our strategic long-range warheads, twenty thousand as against ten thousand. Their purpose is to make it easy to escalate from a conventional war in some part of the world to a nuclear war by providing small steps—steps which do not touch the United States, but which would not be seen as equally "small" from the point of view of the Germans, or the French, or the Italians—from a major conventional war up to the long-range strategic nuclear exchange. In fact, tactical nuclear weapons make it very hard to avoid turning a conventional war into a nuclear war, since they are weapons of last resort, so to speak. If the going gets really bad, there are always tactical nuclear weapons at hand, and that is what you turn to before getting wiped out.

This same function, gradual and supposedly controlled escalation of nuclear warfare—using nuclear weapons to hit targets other than cities—is the rationale behind the whole new generation of strategic nuclear weapons now in development and production. This applies to the Trident II submarine-based missile, which will be far more accurate than necessary for use just against cities; the Mobile MX ICBM, which will be a counterforce weapon; the Cruise missile, which increases our warheads beyond any conceivable use against cities; and the neutron bomb, which is intended to facilitate escalation from a conventional war to a nuclear war. Not one of the new advances being made at this time is based on reinforcing our ability to deter an "out-of-the-blue" nuclear attack against our cities by increasing our capability to reply to it. In fact, we have had that capability for twenty years. The advances that are now being made are based on increasing the likelihood of a conventional war becoming nuclear. Supposedly, these advances are to deter conventional war. However, using nuclear weapons in this way means a permanent nuclear weapons arms race and increased risk of nuclear warfare.

The rationales behind both our strategic and our conventional arms involve foreign-policy issues: concerns about which governments are going to run which areas of the world; who is going to maintain control by what means. It is the same thing we heard earlier about arms sales. In fact, I see the arms race as having three levels of attempts to exert political influence—levels increasingly dangerous from the point of view of the industrialized world. First, there are the arms sales to the Third World, dangerous by themselves. Add to this the conventional forces of the United States, Europe, the Soviet Union, China, and Japan—making possible a confrontation that would make World War II seem pale by comparison. And finally, the tactical nuclear weapons put power politics under the shadow of strategic nuclear warfare. All of this is directed, not at defense, but at hegemony, competition, and control.

Arms-Reduction Efforts

With that outline in mind, what can we do about reducing these weapons?

It is worth remembering that between 1945 and 1960, there were negotiations in the United Nations on what was called "general and complete" disarmament. That meant that the way to disarm was for all countries to get rid of all their arms at once, through negotiations. The theory was that no one would be able to get rid of *anything* unless everybody got rid of *everything*. Looking back at the record of the arms race at that time, I question the sincerity of those negotiations.

In the 1960s we turned to "partial" arms control, again with international negotiations. The prime examples of this are the SALT negotiations on strategic arms, and another forum that we have not been hearing as much about, the Mutual and Balanced Force Reduction (MBFR) negotiations. MBFR is meant to reduce the NATO (American and West European) and Warsaw Pact conventional forces, which together account for about 60 percent of world military spending. But the way the negotiations have been going—the fact that many people have not even heard of them— indicates how far we are from putting pressure on the government to make real cuts in arms and not just give us another cosmetic agreement. What is actually going on in MBFR is very similar to what is going on in SALT. The existing situation is being codified, and the parties are agreeing to go on as they have for the last twenty years, without any real reductions.

The failure of these partial negotiations, following the earlier failure of the "general and complete" negotiations, has led many people in the United States, and perhaps elsewhere, to think about unilateral initiatives or cutbacks. There are four competing and complementary approaches that people are talking about right now.

The first of these is what we in the Boston Study Group have proposed in our book, *The Price of Defense*. What we have tried to do is discriminate between weapons which are more defensively oriented and weapons which we see as hegemonically oriented and less useful for real defense against the Soviet Union—either as a basic deterrent to nuclear war or in a major confrontation with Soviet conventional forces in Europe. We suggest keeping the defensively oriented weapons and getting rid of the others, since they do not contribute to our defense against the Soviet Union, and getting rid of them will in no way endanger our security. We propose to phase out all nuclear weapons geared to war-fighting purposes; virtually all tactical nuclear weapons which increase the likelihood of escalation from conventional to nuclear war; and nearly all of the intervention- ary forces—the aircraft carriers, the amphibious assault ships, the Marines and the light Army divisions.

This is a very radical proposal in comparison with current American military spending; yet it still does not touch the heart of the rationale for our conventional arms, which is the defense of Western Europe. The second approach, therefore, is to focus on the European situation. It suggests substantially reducing the U.S. commitment there.

A third approach is more sweeping: Ban all nuclear arms. This approach addresses the worst problem, but it gives no attention to the high costs of conventional weapons or to the interlocking rationales for the nuclear and conventional arms. The reason that it is so hard to get rid of our nuclear weapons is that political leaders are counting on them to deter another World War II in Europe. Keeping nuclear weapons to deter conventional war is a very dangerous policy which the politicians believe is going to work because they do not think that there will be a nuclear war.

A fourth approach is to ban conventional arms sales to the Third World. Like banning nuclear arms, this involves only one end of the spectrum of weaponry. Linking conventional arms and human rights can command widespread public support. Still, it must be combined with other measures if we are to reduce the military budget or halt the technological arms race.

DEFENSE POLICY ALTERNATIVES

Earl C. Ravenal

It is necessary to begin by countering some mistaken assumptions that are common among my colleagues in the peace movement. Wrong analysis can lead to ineffective remedies, and I think that we are all interested in doing something effective to reverse the arms race. So we have to ask ourselves, where is this money going that is being spent on defense? What are the forces for?

The Carter Administration has requested $126 billion for the 1979 defense budget, and probably in fiscal 1980 the request will be for $138–139 billion, an increase which will consist of about $4 billion in so-called "real increases" over last year and $8–9 billion of inflation. Of that $126 billion for the present year 1979, about 80 percent or $101 billion is going to general purpose forces—conventional forces plus tactical nuclear weapons (which unfortunately are considered conventional by our military establishment). These forces are designed for the forward defense of various regions of the world to support America's military alliances and to intervene in other countries where our government sees the so-called national interest at stake. The other 20 percent of the defense budget, $25 billion, goes toward strategic nuclear forces which are designed to "deter" (in the

EARL C. RAVENAL is with the Institute for Policy Studies. A Professor of International Relations, Georgetown University, he is a former Defense Department official and author of *Never Again: Learning from America's Foreign Policy Failures; Foreign Policy in an Uncontrollable World;* and *Beyond the Balance of Power* (forthcoming).

broad sense of the word) the Soviet Union, although some of those forces are designed very much for war-fighting purposes as well as for deterrence—an increasing and very unfortunate tendency in our strategic nuclear arms arsenal.

What comes out of this brief comparison of percentages of our force structure is that the most dangerous weapons in the world, and those most immoral in their contemplated use, are not, however, the most expensive. They are not nearly as large a portion of our defense spending and our force structure as are the conventional forces. So if we are looking for a two-pronged effort, first to eliminate the possibility of nuclear war, and second to scale down the amount of effort and resources that are going toward the purchase of arms in general, then we have to look very seriously at the conventional area, as well as the nuclear area.

Weapons—Good and Bad

Another point worth noting in this context is that all nuclear weapons are not equally bad. I have found, working within the peace movement, that there is a tendency, which is not helpful to our efforts, to consider all nuclear weapons—indeed in many cases all

Pearl Williams-Jones's rendition of "You'll Never Walk Alone" brought down the house during the liturgy.

weapons—as equally bad, and to call for indiscriminate across-the-board cuts.

This might be proper as our ultimate objective, but when it comes to our pinpointed attacks on individual arms proposals being considered in Congress or floated by the Executive Branch, we sometimes dissipate our efforts by being indiscriminate in our criticism.

For instance, we deal too often in sheer numbers, talking about overkill in terms of simple megatonnage. We total up the megatonnage that is floating around in the arsenals of all the nuclear powers in the world, and somehow we consider one megaton as bad as another. But this is not the way to be effective in the contemporary arms debate. Rather, the weight, enthusiasm, and moral fervor of the peace movement have to be more focused, weapons system by weapons system, force by force, defense dollar by defense dollar. The point is that just getting rid of anything will not have an equally effective result. It makes a difference what arms are eliminated first as a matter of priority and what arms proposals are forestalled.

For instance, many of us spent a good deal of effort fighting the B-1, and we were successful for a brief time. But the B-1 is not nearly as evil, provocative, destabilizing, or dangerous a system as the MX; so lots of time and effort were lost. The B-1, in a sense, is an extremely expensive toy for the Air Force. It is not a destabilizing or provocative weapon, but rather a distinctly second-strike weapon system. Moreover, most of the effort, enthusiasm, and fervor that went into the campaign to cancel the B-1 are lost now, because the administration is making moves to launch the "son of B-1," whatever that might be—a stretched version of some intermediate-range aircraft, or perhaps something that will look very much like the B-1 itself but will be labeled B-2 or B-3.

During the brief time that I was at the Pentagon in the late 1960s, I could see that the advanced manned bomber has had a long history. The B-1 was by no means the first weapon system devoted to that particular strategic purpose. There had been the so-called AMSA, and there had been the B-70, followed by the B-1, and then the FB-111, and now there is the stretched version of that, which is the FB-111H; and tomorrow there will be something else.

Another example is the Trident I Missile (and I'm not talking about the submarine). This system is also not as bad a weapon as the MX. The MX, which is the proposed follow-on, land-based intercontinental ballistic missile, is particularly evil because of its high yield, its many warheads, and its extreme accuracy. That combination of effects and capabilities is bound to destabilize the already fragile "balance of terror," particularly in a crisis, because those are precisely the weapons that the Soviet Union might fear would be used by the United States in a first strike against their own missiles, prompting them to have a much more itchy nuclear trigger finger.

I also want to mention air-launched cruise missiles as another example. These are not as good a first-strike weapon as ground-launched cruise missiles, because in order for an air-launched cruise missile to get within striking range of the Soviet Union, it has to be flown there for ten or twelve hours, which gives everybody plenty of warning. On the other hand, a ground-launched, maneuverable cruise missile launched from the soil of West Germany could indeed be used as a first-strike weapon. So we have to become knowledgeable about the terms of the contemporary debate in order to be effective and in order to place priorities on the kinds of proposals—some of them very dangerous, some of them extremely expensive but not so dangerous—that are being launched by the Executive Branch.

The Soviet Threat

We should also realize that most of the defense budget goes toward our military alliances in the world and toward the shoring up of so-called "proxy powers" that are supposedly willing to do the bidding of the American government in stabilizing various regions of the world. The obvious case is Iran, which had been seen, at least since the Nixon administration and even before that, as an American proxy in the Persian Gulf.

Also included in these general-purpose forces are forces for the repression of various revolutionary groups in the Third World. Of course these forces are overlapping. It takes not only careful analysis, but a good deal of judgment as well, to tell which forces are for the defense of alliances—particularly NATO—and which forces might be used primarily against Third-World factions and revolutionary movements.

Another point I want to make might be contentious, but I think it has to be given weight in designing our attack on the defense budget and on militarism: In the eyes of our defense planners and our foreign-policy makers, the Soviet Union is to be taken seriously. My point is that these people might be quite wrong in assessing the Soviet threat. There might be exaggeration and even a bit of hyperbole in describing, from year to year—as is done in the Secretary of Defense reports to Congress—the power, extent, and intensity of the Soviet buildup. People can differ in the way they measure the Soviet threat, in their interpretations of Soviet motives and purposes. But what we have to realize is that the high level of American defense spending these days and the large annual increases in military spending are generally attributable to certain perceptions of the Soviet challenge in various regions of the world.

The immediate concern might be the perceived Soviet challenge in Europe; or Soviet ambitions—what our policy makers usually consider Soviet "opportunism"—in the Third World, or in perhaps the "Second-and-a-half World," the Persian Gulf, and other developed and fairly wealthy Third-World countries; or defending the sea lanes against what they see as a challenge by the Soviet Navy, which has made great strides since the time of Stalin when they had nothing but a coastal defense force. It is now a blue-water navy that is capable of cutting the sea lanes between the United States and its allies in the world and interdicting efforts the United States might make to reinforce its own and allied forces in a major European confrontation.

All of these things are true, whatever interpretation we entertain. The policy makers take the Soviet threat seriously, and right or wrong, this is the primary motive behind the increase—after several years of leveling off (ironically during the Nixon administration)— which began in the late Republican administrations of the mid-1970s and has continued under the Carter administration. Whether correctly conceived or misconceived, there is an urgent desire to keep up with the Soviet Union in certain regions of the world, particularly Central Europe. It is not just paranoia, nor merely the operation of the military-industrial complex. It is not just waste and inefficiency in our defense efforts, or sheer mindlessness or momentum. And it is not some conspiracy or excuse for imposing a kind of native fascism on the United States—although I must say that many forms of repression of individual liberties and many of the perversions of our Constitution and betrayals of individual rights in this country, as well as the distortions of our economy and society, are the *result* of this misplaced emphasis on national security.

In other words, these abuses that we experience in our domestic society, economically, legally, and constitutionally, are results of a misplaced orientation toward national security; but they are not the purpose of these "national security" efforts. People within the peace movement must realize that those who consider defense budgets and forces year in and year out, whether in the Executive Branch or in Congress, are absolutely sincere about the strategic purpose of increasing these arms budgets, and that is the ground on which they have to be attacked. The issue has to be confronted directly. It is too easy to say that this is mindlessness or paranoia, without a reason. If there were no reason, then this phenomenon might have gone away years ago. The trouble is that there *is* a reason. It might be the wrong reason, but there is a reason; and we have to confront that reason.

Linkage

We should keep in mind that, for all our fears about the possible use of nuclear weapons in the world, it remains extremely unlikely that they will be used, particularly in a scenario where one side simply contrives to attack the other. That is not the way the dynamics of nuclear confrontation work. Very often we talk about nuclear weapons as if simply increasing their number will lead to war. That might be the end result, but you have to trace the intermediate linkage between an increase in arms—particularly nuclear arms—and the probability of war; and there is a lot of intermediate linkage. For example, that linkage consists of confrontations that the United States might have with the Soviet Union or with Soviet allies in various regions of the world. Those need to be looked at because they are the triggers. The rest is simply tinder; what you need is a spark.

Thus, the peace movement has to look beyond weapons arsenals, to the circumstances or sparks that occur in various regions of the world and how American alliance commitments provide the linkage or the trigger that can detonate a nuclear war. We have to look at the kinds of obligations to which we have chained ourselves, because these are likely to trigger a war. Both hawks and doves are mistaken in this matter. The hawks would persuade us that Soviet increases in weapons are likely to touch off a war. The doves, of course, talk about American increases in weapons, as if by themselves they are likely to precipitate the Third World War.

When we recognize this series of linkages, we find the reason why both this country and the Soviet Union can disarm substantially within the basic framework of disincentives against using nuclear weapons. Even without arguing for the complete stability of the nuclear balance at this point (which is far from what I am arguing— there are many elements of instability, and they are being made worse by these counter-force weapons that both sides are devising), there is still a substantial disincentive against using the vast arsenals being amassed by both sides; and conversely, there is considerable reason and opportunity for disarming within that basic framework of confrontation.

Another point is that disarmament, especially nuclear

disarmament, does not necessarily lead to greater strategic stability in the world. It is too easy to make that assumption, that all good things run in the same direction; but they do not. There are hard choices and trade-offs that have to be made. It is not only conceivable, but quite likely, that if the United States were to scale down its arsenals of weapons and discontinue its arms transfers, certain regions of the world would become less stable. And other nations that are currently U.S. clients would move to create their own defense capabilities— larger forces, indigenous weapons-production capabilities, even nuclear arsenals. In fact, I would say that more nations would move to compensate for an American withdrawal of arms support than would be encouraged by our example to diminish their own arsenals. But that is a decision that would have to be left to other nations. It does not furnish an excuse for us to continue arming two-thirds of the world.

Entangling Alliances

Another point is that strategic nuclear forces are integrally related to our alliances, particularly NATO. Many people believe that American defense planners have invented certain kinds of nuclear weapons for the diabolical purpose of exterminating large numbers of Third-World people. Friends of mine have argued rather eloquently that the neutron bomb in particular was designed specifically and covertly to use in Third-World situations. But I doubt that this is true. If it were, the situation might be *less* dangerous than it is, for Europe is clearly the theater where most of these advanced weapons are designed to be used, and Europe is the situation most likely to touch off the use of these mass weapons of horror. Indeed, most of the American nuclear posture derives, not from any immediate fear of the Soviet Union—they do not have any great incentive to use their nuclear weapons against the United States just out of the blue—but rather from our NATO commitment.

The desire to extend the so-called "nuclear umbrella" of the United States over other nations to protect them from other kinds of attack is called "extended deterrence," as opposed to "pure deterrence." The commitment to NATO, in particular, implies an American first use of nuclear weapons. And that is why even the most benign American defense planners that we have seen over the last few years—even a Paul Warnke—could refuse to contemplate a declaration of "no first use," and why they could argue for incorporating within the SALT II agreements the continuation of American efforts to develop the MX strategic missile, which is a counterforce weapon. Even the most benign and dovish members of any administration see that if we remain committed to the fate of NATO, then we are also committed to the first use of nuclear weapons, and by the same logic to the development of counterforce strategic nuclear weapons. Of course, those are the only kinds of nuclear weapons that conceivably could be used first, since obviously a first strike must contemplate the destruction of an enemy's missiles, not the destruction of its cities.

So we have the connection: NATO and our military alliances in general imply some of the most evil aspects of our strategic nuclear posture. The corollary to this is that any unilateral American disarmament, which I happen to favor very strongly, and any nuclear restraint, which I would urge most passionately, will have the effect of weakening America's military alliances. In fact, these actions would dissolve whatever faith governments, such as West Germany and others, might have in the guarantees of the United States. Allies and other countries might be inspired to become more independent in their foreign policy and even to acquire or expand their national nuclear forces.

Deterrence and Alliance

In general, there have been few changes in America's foreign policy from one administration to another since World War II. There has been a sort of "paradigm" that has characterized American foreign and military policy for the last thirty years, a pattern of deterrence and alliance. Deterrence means, of course, "extended deterrence," and alliance means "forward defense." Actually, as we have seen, these are two sides of the same coin. True, there have been oscillations within this paradigm, leading us to believe that policies were being changed. Truman and Acheson, for instance, engaged in a vast expansion of our conventional forces, while Eisenhower and Dulles, believing in "more bang for the buck," got us into doctrines of massive retaliation. Kennedy and McNamara brought in flexible response. Then Nixon and Kissinger brought the Nixon Doctrine with them, and we drifted back to greater reliance on nuclear deterrence, in a kind of sleight-of-hand. Now President Carter and Secretary of Defense Harold Brown have renewed the emphasis on conventional forces and NATO. But there has never been a complete policy reversal. Each administration has brought the baggage of the previous administration along with it, while altering the emphasis slightly, but all within that basic paradigm of deterrence and alliance that we have seen since the end of World War II.

Perhaps a related point is that "everybody" favors arms control. It is the liberal solution to all evils. The trouble is that arms control means formal, reciprocal arms-limitation agreements, principally with the Soviet Union, and this kind of arms control has not in the past and will not in the future lead to serious disarmament. It will not obviate expensive new weapons systems; it will not obviate destabilizing and provocative new weapons systems; and it will not obviate future confrontations with either the Soviet Union or other nations and forces in the world. Of course, we would all be better off with SALT II, and we must hope that SALT II (and SALT III) are negotiated, ratified, and come into force. We would be much worse off without them. But you cannot draw the converse conclusion. These agreements will not do us very much good, and we should not expect too much from them.

The upshot of all this is that the present defense postures and budgets, national strategies, and foreign policies are deeply imbedded in the way the United States has done business for three decades, and they have been adopted and perpetuated for a variety of reasons— good or bad, right or wrong—but not for *no* reason. Unfortunately, the effects have been harmful and occasionally disastrous. We have had several limited wars, frequent interventions, confrontations, and crises, along with the continuing high cost of defense preparations, the distraction of government and society from more constructive purposes, demoralization—in the literal sense of the word—of generations of American leadership, and the constant specter of nuclear war. So the question arises: If these elements are so deeply imbedded in our policy, and they have had such disastrous, deleterious effects, what can we do about them?

The answer is that we must change our policy drastically. *But we must know what has to be changed.* There is no simple solution. It is not a matter of cutting some Gordian knot. We have to know the risks and prospective "losses" internationally. More specifically, the large and unilateral cuts that I favor in our strategic and conventional forces and budgets—I think we can cut from 40 to 45 percent of our forces and budgets and save over one-half trillion dollars in the next decade—will have the effect of uncoupling the American nuclear arsenal from the defense of other regions of the world. We must accept the fact that, if we make these kinds of cuts, we can no longer plan to build forces to defend other regions of the world. We must also change our nuclear doctrine to include a policy of "no first use" under any circumstances and no deliberate targeting of civilians, even in retaliation. And we must eliminate the destabilizing elements of our strategic nuclear forces.

However, we must realize that, if we do these things, we are going to see the evolution of a very different kind of world, a very different international system. There will be "penalties"; our alliances will be damaged, particularly in Western Europe; and some people whom many have regarded as friends in the world will have to adopt measures of self-reliance. There will be some thrusts or probes by the Soviet Union, and our government will have to minimize them because we might have lost our ability to counter them. Even the deterrence of some nuclear attacks will be marginally diminished. Our government will have to get out of the business of distinguishing between "good" and "bad" causes in the world and supporting so-called "good" causes with arms and promises of force. (We won't be able to "knock over," as George McGovern put it, a Cambodia, or a Uganda, or even, I must say in all candor, a South Africa.)

I believe that most of these "penalties" would actually be blessings. Others might disagree. But at least we should be clear about the costs as well as the benefits, the pains as well as the blessings.

THE ARMS RACE: WHO BENEFITS?

Michael Clark

We have heard that the arms race is probably just contributing to our insecurity. And we have heard that the arms race is probably costing us hundreds of thousands of jobs. And we have heard that the arms race is wasting limited resources that could be used for meeting basic human needs. And we have heard that it is not in the best long-term interests of defense workers. And we have heard that it is probably not even in the best interests of citizens in the various garrison states around the world.

So my question to myself and to each of you is: If it is in nobody's interest to keep this thing going, then why hasn't the momentum slowed? If it is in nobody's interest to keep this thing going, why haven't the upward trends begun to level off? If it is in nobody's interest to keep this thing going, why hasn't it collapsed of its own weight? Surely it must be in somebody's interest?

The Corporate Giants

The plane that dropped the bomb on Hiroshima was called the Enola Gay. It was a B-29 Super Fortress, manufactured by the Boeing Corporation. And while Joseph Stalin, who was supposed to be intimidated by the bomb, is long gone; and while Dwight Eisenhower, who had second thoughts about the bomb, is long gone; and while Harry Truman, who thought the bomb was the greatest

MICHAEL CLARK is on the staff of the Interfaith Center on Corporate Responsibility, and associate, Disarmament Program, Riverside Church.

thing in history, is long gone; the Boeing Corporation lives on.

While administrations have come and gone, and while strategic doctrines have been formulated and reformulated, and while enemies and allies have switched places in our global/political perspective, the military-industrial complex has remained vital and has outlived them all—intact, alive, and well. In 1977, the military procurement budget reached an all-time high of $50 billion. Tens of thousands of contracts went to every state in the union, but the top 100 contractors accounted for 68 percent of the $50 billion in sales. And the top ten of those top 100 accounted for 30 percent of the $50 billion. Those top ten, if anyone needs to be reminded, are McDonnell-Douglas, Lockheed, United Technologies, Boeing, General Electric, Rockwell International, Grumman, General Dynamics, Hughes Aircraft, and Northrop.

Many of these contractors are increasingly dependent upon military work for their very economic existence. In fact, some are becoming increasingly dependent on arms exports for their continued economic viability. One drastic example is McDonnell-Douglas, based in St. Louis, where it employs 30,000 workers and gets fifty-eight cents of each federal dollar which comes into that city. Last year, 73 percent of their sales and 95 percent of their profits were military related. So the military market is booming, the contracts continue to increase, and military production continues to be one of the most profitable types of work that any corporation can undertake.

When one goes to the corporate management of the major multi-national corporations, as we have done at the Interfaith Center on Corporate Responsibility during the last three years, one finds that corporate management is perfectly willing to admit its dependency on military contracts. We find that corporate management is prepared to admit its involvement in the manufacture of various weapons, both nuclear and conventional. What we do not find, however, is any willingness on the part of those corporations or that management to admit that they have anything to do with the level of military spending which currently exists in this country.

Whether it is the chairman of Northrop, or the general council of Textron, or a half-dozen vice-presidents of General Electric, or public relations officials from Bendix, it does not make any difference. The response to this issue is always the same: (1) It is the task of the federal government to determine U.S. foreign policy and to implement that foreign policy by military means. (2) It is the task of U. S. corporations to meet those needs. (3) It is inappropriate for

U.S. Arms Control and Disarmament Agency's Thomas Halsted listening to a point from Soviet Embassy's Yuri Kapralov during convocation break.

corporations to have an independent judgment about the kind of work which they are being asked to perform. That response is easily enough explained.

Less easily explained are the things which not only contradict this fiction put forward by the multinationals, but also undermine it and show it to be a lie. Less easily explained are the tens of millions of dollars worth of lobbying done by those very corporations to insure a continued channel of profits and sales in the military sector. In a recent issue of the *New York Times* there was an article about President Carter's foreign military sales policy in which perhaps the most essential point was that Carter is trying to balance off criticism at home and abroad with the "heavy pressure" being applied by domestic armaments producers.

It is easily enough explained that the corporations have nothing to do with foreign policy or the creation of that policy, but it is not quite so easy to explain the situation which exists regarding the transfer of personnel back and forth between the Department of Defense and the top echelons of management. It is not only feasible and legal, but absolutely true, that some people at the top levels of the Defense Department leave their jobs on Friday afternoon at five o'clock, retire, and begin working for Boeing or Northrop at nine o'clock Monday morning. It is less easy to explain what that says about the distinctions which the corporations like to draw between themselves and the creation of public policy. It is also less easily explained when one takes a look at their public relations budgets, meant not only to influence Congress, but also to create a climate in this country favoring continued military contracts.

One of the prime examples occurred in the late 1960s during the debate on the ABM system, when paid advertisements appeared in newspapers around the country saying that 84 percent of the American people were in favor of an ABM system because they felt we needed it for our national defense. But when one took a look at the list of signatories and cosponsors of the advertisements, one found that many were contractors for the ABM system. So all of this is not so easily explained if one wishes to draw distinctions between creating public policy and merely filling orders.

It is also difficult to understand and explain the profusion of arms bazaars, both here and abroad, during which hundreds of manufacturers and thousands of interested people are brought together for a few days to examine the newest wares in the corporate marketplace. And finally, even more difficult to explain is the fact that sometimes the lobbying, and the pressure, and the arms bazaars are not enough. As we look at the issue of questionable overseas payments over the last three years, we find that the one industry whose record of using bribes and kickbacks overseas is literally 100 percent is the armaments industry.

All of these things point toward one goal, and it is important for us to recognize that goal and to challenge it at every opportunity. That goal is the attempt of private corporations to equate their own economic self-interest with the national interest of this country. I know of no example on record of any multinational corporation ever lobbying to reduce the military budget or to abolish a particular weapons system. Even when debate has been raging in the Congress, in the Executive Branch, and in the country at large, the corporations have found it possible to remain silent.

Arms Bazaar

I would like to read something which I think shows clearly what a difficult business this is. In fact, I think even those who benefit and profit from the continued arms race realize that it is a dirty business. I am quoting from a flyer which is called "Defense Technology '79"— an arms bazaar scheduled for Chicago's O'Hare Exposition Center in February of 1979.[1] On the second page, in print almost too small to see, the sponsors of "Defense '79" say this: "It is stressed that the conference is not designed to stimulate international arms sales, but is presented to facilitate discussion and understanding on the broadest possible range of strategic and defense subjects."

Now, in somewhat larger print on the first two pages of the leaflet one reads this:

> Defense Technology '79 . . . Where can you find thousands of defense buyers from the West and Third World? At Defense Technology '79— O'Hare International Exposition Center, Chicago, Illinois, U.S.A. Never before has there been a gathering like this. Defense policymakers and procurement officers from throughout the West and Third World are coming to Chicago. They'll be at the O'Hare International Exposition Center, an outstanding facility offering 200,000 square feet of exposition space, for a series of more than 100 seminars on key topics in international defense. The staff is in touch with more than 40,000 of the leading defense decision-makers throughout the West and Third World. Each of these individuals is being personally contacted to insure the maximum attendance possible at this exciting event.
>
> Defense Technology '79 has been conceived and executed by the combined efforts of the most experienced professionals in the defense field.

And then under the heading: "Some space still available," it closes . . .

> Every leading firm of the defense field will be a part of Defense Technology '79. If your country is involved in any aspect of defense, you cannot afford to miss this opportunity. From multinationals to smaller suppliers of components and subsystems, defense firms of all sizes and persuasions will be attending this show. Act now and become a part of the world's most outstanding defense marketing experience.

I would like to suggest that one of the hopes we should share in this conference is that, some day, the United States Supreme Court will broaden its interpretation of obscenity to include such advertising copy as this, and I look forward to working with each and every one of you to hasten that day.

[1] "Defense Technology '79," Update #1, Conference Management Corporation, 411 West Putnam Avenue, Greenwood, CT 06830.

THE ARMS RACE: WHO PAYS?

Betty G. Lall

While the arms budget in this country is often cited as being a declining share of the Gross National Product, it remains the largest single item in the budget, outside of income maintenance. Our defense budget is estimated to be approximately 64 percent of all the controllable costs in the budget, which is to say that if you took the full budget of the United States and eliminated permanent expenditures, such as interest, income maintenance, Social Security, and so on, you would be left with the controllable part of the budget, and 64 percent of that is the defense budget. This means to me that wasteful, unnecessary, and provocative programs in the defense budget ought to be important areas for cuts if the president's goal of cutting inflation by reducing government spending is serious, but so far this has not been the case.

Dubious Benefits

Perhaps the most important part of the defense budget—in terms of who benefits—is the approximately $40 billion spent in the private sector for military research and development, and procurement of major weapons. The research and development portion accounts for over $12 billion of this, and it is increasing every year.

Literally thousands and thousands of firms get this money, but

BETTY G. LALL is with the New York State School of Industrial and Labor Relations, Cornell University, and was a member of the U.S. Delegation, Geneva Disarmament Conference (1962). She is author of *Prosperity Without Guns.*

most of the contracts go to relatively few firms which are all located in a few states, so that the defense industry is very concentrated. California, in particular, has been far ahead, with about 23 percent of all defense contracts, although New York, Connecticut, Massachusetts, New Jersey, Pennsylvania, Texas, Missouri, and Washington also get a large share of defense contracts in the private sector. In addition, there are states, such as Arizona and New Mexico, that do not receive large contracts in terms of total amount spent, but in which this total amount is a very high proportion of that state's income. In other words, there are two ways of looking at defense procurement disbursement by states. One is to see where the bulk of the money goes, and the other is to see how it is used in states where defense spending is a major proportion of the economy.

Since defense contracting has become more capital- rather than labor-intensive, every billion dollars of defense spending goes less and less to pay people and more to "things." The money that is spent on people goes to highly paid scientists, engineers, and administrators, while fewer and fewer segments of the defense pie go to production workers and lower-paid white-collar employees. Therefore, defense spending is not the best use of money if one major objective in this society is to try to maintain high employment.

Another large chunk of the defense budget—on the order of $30–40 billion—goes for operation and maintenance of our bases, depots, and other facilities. These are located in every state, and since they mean a politically acceptable distribution of funds in the best "pork-barrel" tradition, these activities encourage widespread support for the defense budget because there is something in the way of base locations for everyone. There are even many cases, particularly in small communities, where the military facility is one of the key economic aspects of that locality. When base closings are announced in such communities, a great crisis results. Adequate legislation has not yet been developed to deal with such a crisis.

Finally, in terms of who benefits from defense spending, a substantial amount of the military budget goes for the pensions of military officers and enlisted personnel—a source of much criticism today, in and out of Congress. Military pensions are very high compared to their civilian counterparts, and many retired personnel continue to be paid full military pensions even when they return to active work as civilians on the federal payroll. This is a status not permitted other retirees receiving Social Security benefit payments, so we have a double standard here—something that the rest of the population under Social Security cannot have. There is likely to be some congressional action in this area, but we do not know how extensive it will be.

Costs of Defense

Turning now to who pays for the military budget, I want to examine the linkage between the military and other sectors. Our government is financed at the federal level primarily by the personal income tax. Corporation taxes have been declining markedly as a factor in our whole federal revenue. The largest part of the federal income tax dollar goes to the Department of Defense. If we care about how our hard-earned money is spent, the first place to look is the Department of Defense; that is where our money goes. And when we examine what happens to our money in the defense sector, we find some disturbing factors.

First, defense funds are contracted for under less competitive conditions than almost any other segment of the economy, because the defense industry is so concentrated that it has become more and more monopolistic. Fewer firms compete for esoteric new weapons systems, meaning that there is an insufficient competitive structure in the defense area to hold down costs. Secondly, defense spending is more inflationary than other sectors of government spending, because so many of the private funds go to pay highly priced personnel who are nonproductive. We have to keep reminding ourselves that this money is going for nonproductive purposes—a highly inflationary situation compared to other activities in the federal sector which we may or may not want to pay for, but which are at least productive and which keep feeding productive activity into the marketplace.

Thirdly, there is great doubt that so much money for research and development is really needed. In my view, cuts in the military budget should come from this sector as well as from procurement. The military research and development sector feeds the arms race because it is now a qualitative arms race. But this is the area that is seldom looked at critically in Congress or the research arena.

Although we know that much defense money is wasted, that it fuels inflation more than other government spending, and that it encourages monopolistic rather than competitive bidding, of particular importance to the average taxpayer is the price paid in terms of the quality of daily life. In urban centers there is not enough housing, and the inflation rate in the housing industry is growing. Most people—especially the elderly—are paying more each year for medical help, and our government refuses to do what all other industrialized countries except South Africa have done, namely, create a national health care system.

Furthermore, most cities suffer from the huge burden of paying part of the cost of welfare because our federal government refuses to accept the responsibility of paying the full cost of welfare. Most cities suffer from crime, but the federal government will not allocate enough funds to train and put young people to work, and they are the ones who commit most of the street crime. Funds for mass transit, improvement of environmental quality, increased research on renewal energy sources—these are all inadequate. And finally, the United States ranks ninth or tenth among industrialized states in terms of economic aid to developing nations for their efforts to deal with poverty, disease, and hunger. This is all part of the price we pay. These are the things we cannot get because the government keeps cutting them in order to fight inflation, instead of cutting the key inflationary force, which is defense spending.

Action for the Future

The focus of stopping the high cost of the arms race must start primarily at home. Negotiations are not enough. We have to have closer public as well as congressional scrutiny of the military budget. Ordinarily, hearings on these questions do not command public interest, but if every church group, student group, faculty group, women's group, and social service group demanded to be heard by the Armed Services Committees of the House and Senate, they would have to listen to us. If they refused, we would ask other congressional committees to set up *ad hoc* hearings to let the people speak on the military budget. This has not been done, and it ought to be done.

A second focus should be greater citizen scrutiny of candidates who run for federal office, in terms of their views and knowledge of defense and national security issues. A few months ago, I ran for Congress in order to make some of the very points that we are making here, such as linking the dangers of the military budget with the need for domestic programs. Many groups interview candidates to assess their views for endorsement or just to know where they stand. But I can attest to the fact that on the East Side and part of the West Side of New York City, not one foreign policy group asked candidates relevant questions. Here is an opportunity for groups to have candidates come before them to answer ahead of time how they stand on the defense budget, on national security questions, and so forth, and it is an opportunity that we should not lose.

Finally, we need to do a lot more disciplining of our own

activities—getting together, knowing where we are going. We ought to insist, as we do our lobbying and place our priorities, that every arms control agreement have economic savings built into it. As far as I know, only one agreement has had that. SALT II, as important as it might be, will include no provision for economic saving. Part of the problem of who pays and who benefits is that arms negotiations are structured so that there is no economic saving. The spending for arms is encouraged to continue, and that is something we ought to curtail.

NUCLEAR WAR IS THINKABLE AND POSSIBLE

George Wald

Some of my physicist friends are starry-eyed over the prospect of radio communication with what they call "advanced technological societies in outer space." I think all that is just another nightmare, and we fight about it. But nightmare or not, they have been listening for a generation now without hearing anything meaningful. And the thought is gaining ground that perhaps there are no advanced technological societies in outer space. Perhaps they self-destruct when they approach our stage of development, as our society is threatening to do.

Let me say at once that I reject all of that. There is no natural law that anticipates the self-extinction of advanced technological societies. What we see happening is the result of the special structures of our particular society—the exploitative forms on both sides of the Iron Curtain. On our side it is the search for profit, and on the other side, the pursuit of the shibboleth of production. But we should recognize by now that the society whose ultimate goal is production ends up being not very different from one whose ultimate goal is profit.

In 1976 we were celebrating—in what has come to be our tawdry American way—the bicentennial of American independence. Certainly, American independence was an interesting event, but minor compared to something else that was happening at the same

GEORGE WALD is Professor Emeritus, at Harvard University, and a Nobel Laureate in biochemistry.

time—the Industrial Revolution. As a scientist, I see things in a rather long perspective: 20 billion years of the universe; 6 billion years of the solar system; 4.7 billion years of the earth; 3 billion years of life on earth; 3 million years of something resembling human life; 10,000 years of civilization. And now a trivial, miserable 200 years of the Industrial Revolution have brought us to the brink of self-extinction.

The industrial use of coal was just beginning two hundred years ago, and the petroleum industry is only one hundred years old. The first petroleum well was dug in western Pennsylvania in 1859, and it took awhile before there was even a modest industry. For the first twenty-five years the gasoline fraction of petroleum was looked upon as a useless and dangerous by-product. The only question was how to get rid of it before it blew up. Then Henry Ford started to mass-produce cars, and that marked the first use of gasoline. Today, the world is full of people hardly able to imagine how civilization could go on without gasoline. And now we are being told that we cannot live without nuclear power. But the reality is: We cannot live *with* nuclear power.

Disarmament—Not Arms Control

The realities of armaments are terrifying. Ten years ago, nuclear weapons stockpiles in the United States and the Soviet Union had reached the explosive equivalent of 5–15 tons of TNT for every man, woman, and child on earth. That comes to 40–120 tons of TNT for every man, woman, and child, just in the United States and the Soviet Union. A half-hour interchange between the superpowers would be "curtains" for the human race, because we now have stockpiled the explosive equivalent of 15 billion tons of TNT. In this country alone, we have enough stockpiled to obliterate completely every Russian city of over 100,000 people forty times. And the Russians have enough to obliterate every American city of over 100,000 people twenty times. Our nation is making three hydrogen warheads a day— about one thousand a year—and it has been going at that pace for at least the last seven years. It's crazy—unless of course one holds a defense contract, in which case it's business, and the more of it the better.

The word "disarmament" has not appeared in an official American pronouncement or document for a very long time. It has become—to coin a phrase—inoperative. The trouble with the word "disarmament" is that it means something; it means fewer arms. But it has been replaced officially by two completely meaningless terms: "arms control" and "arms limitation." SALT means "Strategic Arms

Limitation Talks." But the terms are completely meaningless. You can control arms up or down. So far, it has always been up, and however far up they go, they will always be "limited." What we have been through is fifteen years of utter frustration in the guise of arms control and arms limitation. It began in 1963 with the Partial Test Ban Treaty, and since then we have had ten bilateral and seven multilateral treaties without even slowing the arms race. All that has happened is that the United States and Soviet Union periodically agree not to do what neither of them had any intention of doing in the first place!

That may sound like a useless exercise, but it has served a very important function: It has completely diffused and frustrated the disarmament movement. All the time we are told, "Delicate negotiations are in progress. Don't rock the boat." Now we are hearing about SALT II, and I want to say right now that it will not be worth having. It will just be the next step in the same frustration. Disarmament has the reputation of being something for the softheaded in this country—for "kooks" and impractical people. Disarmament is politically unacceptable. But the extinction of the human race is thoroughly sound politically.

The late Senator Richard Russell of Georgia once gave a patriotic speech in the Senate in which he spoke of the possibility of a nuclear holocaust. Said Russell, "If we have to get back to Adam and Eve, I want them to be Americans, and I want them on this continent and not in Europe." That kind of criminal insanity goes down as superior wisdom and patriotism. There is a real patriot. We will reduce the American population to a man and a woman, and hope that the woman can be made to conceive. You have to know what you are up against and with whom you are dealing.

The Corporate State

The Pentagon is not the master; it is the servant. Our government is not the master; it too is the servant.

Our masters are the major corporations and the banks. We live in a corporate state—not only our government, but also every government in the free world, which includes the largest number of military dictatorships ever assembled in history. All of the governments are serving that same master in the developed world and even more in the underdeveloped world. They all know that they must make a proper bargain with the big transnational corporations and banks or else their governments will disappear.

Here is another thought: For many years, our country has been a one-party state masquerading as a two-party state. I doubt that anyone can cite an ideological difference between the Republican and Democratic parties. When we had Republican presidents, they found their principal support in the Democratic majority in Congress. And when, as now, we have a Democratic president, he finds that if he gets out of step, his principal opposition comes from that same Democratic majority in Congress. The only effective politics operating in America is corporate politics.

Exxon is the biggest corporation in the world, with sales in 1977 of $58 billion. General Motors is the second biggest corporation in the world, and its 1977 sales worldwide were $53 billion. Sometimes people ask me why we are not conserving fuel since we are supposed to be in a fuel and energy crisis. I have just given the beginnings of an answer.

There are only eighteen nations in the whole world with Gross National Products as big as the annual sales of Exxon or General Motors. They should not be thought of as just businesses; they are major powers. When I say that, one might ask, "Major powers? Do they have armed forces?" Yes, they have *our* armed forces. "Do they have an intelligence network?" Yes, they have the FBI and the CIA. "Do they have a system of control?" Yes, they have our government.

One talks about our armaments program in such terms as statecraft and military strategy—great and noble things. But in reality, it is very largely a business. Killing and destruction are now the biggest business in the world. The military bill in 1977 came to $340 billion. But there is a curious thing about the arms business; not only is it very big, it is also concealed. After a lot of research, I learned that the weapons industry has some surprising components. For example, do not be so naive as to think that a company such as Singer limits itself to making sewing machines. The arms business is a well-hidden business.

Our Role as Citizens

I must confess that I own some stocks, although I don't let that fact affect my sentiments or my actions. I am always fighting the companies in which I hold stock, two of which are Exxon and General Motors. I have never seen, in any of their corporate reports, one single word about defense contracts. However, in a list of the 100 primary defense contractors in this country, General Motors is twenty-fourth and Exxon is thirty-eighth. You have to know whom you are fighting if you are to do anything about the situation.

But what are we to do about it? I think we need to rediscover what it used to mean to be an American. I think we have to take back our country. I think that anybody who is not living politically is hardly living humanly. It was Aristotle who called man a political animal. Politics is not just a dirty game played by some dirty people. Politics is the only means by which complex society can manage to survive. If you are not living politically, you are not living humanly. We are said to be a democracy. I would like all Americans to test their democracy. In part, that would mean no longer buying candidates off the "tube," sold to us by the same people (using the same methods) who sell us toothpaste and soap.

As a professor, I had a lot to do with students in the 1960s. They thought they had to invent a new world, new life-styles, new ways of going about everything—even education. I used to say to them, "You don't have to invent it all, just try to fulfill some of it." And that is our job, to fulfill those wonderful, meaningful words that are not just noises, but need to be clothed with flesh:

"Government of the people, by the people, for the people. . . .
". . . with liberty and justice for all."

DÉTENTE AND DISARMAMENT—U.S.

Thomas Halsted

I come to you as a representative of an administration which reflects many viewpoints regarding the problems being discussed at this conference, but one whose fundamental objective I think all of us share. We may define it in different ways, but basically that objective is to strengthen our security, in its broadest sense. I do not mean a false security based only on growing military might, but one based on the principle that no one is secure if we cannot expect a future free from fear of war or privation.

We do think that we need adequate arms for defense and for deterrence of nuclear war, but endlessly spending our resources on armaments brings us no security, increases the danger we are in, and is likely to lead only to disaster in the end. It is what Paul Warnke has called a "chumps game," to go on spending billions and billions of dollars in a futile effort to try, through arms, to provide the kind of security we can achieve only if we get rid of our arms.

Arms Control Efforts

Over the past two decades or so, successive administrations have sought to curb the world's growing dependence on arms through negotiated arms-control agreements. In the early 1960s, we had the Limited Test Ban Treaty, which of course only led to increased testing

THOMAS HALSTED is with the Office of Public Affairs, U.S. Arms Control and Disarmament Agency, and a member, Arms Control Association; Council on Foreign Relations; International Institute of Strategic Studies.

of nuclear weapons underground. (Some have called it the world's first international clean air act, but other than that, it did not do a great deal to slow the development of new weapons.) We have had the Nuclear Nonproliferation Treaty, which contains promises not yet delivered, and we have had treaties for keeping weapons of mass destruction from outer space and off the seabed.

This administration is engaged in a wide range of negotiations, both bilateral and multilateral, on a variety of arms control efforts. For the first time since the early 1960s, we are working to negotiate a comprehensive test ban treaty. The talks on Mutual and Balanced Force Reductions in Vienna have just had their fifth birthday, and although I cannot say that they have shown a great deal of progress, we are continuing to pursue efforts to reduce the likelihood of conflict in Central Europe. We have had talks with the Soviet Union on ways of controlling, limiting, and hopefully eliminating anti-satellite warfare—we are already into *that* Buck Rogers era. We are talking about chemical and radiological weapons disarmament; we have had some bilateral discussions with the Soviet Union on limiting our military activities in the Indian Ocean; and we are engaged in talks to find ways of curbing the enormously costly and disastrous competition in conventional arms sales around the world. It is these conventional weapons, after all, that are killing people, not the nuclear weapons covered by SALT (our Strategic Arms Limitation Talks).

This administration is putting a very high priority on SALT. We are going around the country talking to people in all walks of life, from varied backgrounds and interests, trying to find out what they think about the U.S./Soviet competition, how to control it, and whether the SALT process that we are engaged in is the right way to go. Some people have been calling this "the selling of SALT," but I hope that, rather than going to the American people as salesmen, we are going more as listeners, because if our arms control efforts do not involve the things that the American people want—if we are only out there lecturing about what we think is best for you—we may find that we are not doing anything good for any of us.

Strategic arms levels have reached awesome heights: some nine thousand strategic nuclear weapons on our side, and nearly five thousand on the Soviet side aimed at one another. We long ago passed the point where we had enough targets for all the weapons we have now built, and yet we keep building more. We have been adding something like three nuclear warheads a day to our strategic weapons arsenal, and the Soviet Union, which started later, followed our lead into the development of one stage after another of these weapons programs. The multiple-warhead program, MIRV, is one in which the Soviets have now started to move very quickly, so that while they had a paltry four thousand strategic weapons aimed at U.S. targets a year ago, they now have nearly five thousand. And so it goes, building up and up, with every one of these nuclear weapons much larger than the 13-kiloton atomic bomb that devastated Hiroshima in 1945.

SALT

The centerpiece of our arms control efforts is SALT. We and the Russians decided at Glassboro, New Jersey, back in 1967, that we ought to find some way to negotiate an end to this enormous buildup of arms. At that time, the levels were much lower than they are now. But we got off to a slow start, because in the summer of 1968, just as talks were scheduled to begin, Soviet tanks moved into Czechoslovakia, and for a variety of political reasons it seemed unwise—perhaps impossible on many levels—to sit down and start talking about strategic arms control.

We finally began the Strategic Arms Limitation Talks in November, 1969, and by May, 1972, we had reached the agreement which became SALT I, the treaty limiting to very low levels—and eventually almost totally eliminating—anti-ballistic missiles, or ABMs. The ABM Treaty was accompanied by an interim agreement on the control of strategic offensive arms—the intercontinental ballistic missiles and the submarine-launched ballistic missiles—that are aimed by our two countries at one another. It did not, however, cover a number of other weapons, such as strategic bombers or the so-called "forward-based" systems, which include the shorter-range weapons that the U.S. and NATO forces have in Western Europe and that the Soviet Union has aimed at targets in Europe (but not at the United States). That interim agreement expired a year ago, although both sides continue to act as though it were still in effect.

In 1974, President Ford and Soviet General Secretary Brezhnev agreed at Vladivostok on what the SALT II Treaty would encompass. Essentially, they set ceilings which, although equal on both sides, were very high—2,400 weapons systems for each side, a "system" consisting of an ICBM missile silo, a submarine launch tube, or a strategic intercontinental bomber. And of all those 2,400 weapons systems, 1,320 could have multiple warheads on them. There were no other controls agreed upon at Vladivostok. In fact, it was not a treaty as much as an agreement to agree; it was a starting point. Many critics claimed that this Vladivostok agreement was potentially good, but that it had in it the seeds of an expanded qualitative arms race. It was not itself a guarantee that we had done anything whatever about really controlling this offensive arms competition. Then the 1976 presidential campaign essentially brought a halt to further serious negotiations, and SALT was largely in limbo.

After the Carter administration took office, a delegation went to Moscow in March, 1977, and presented two alternative plans to the Soviet government. One would have taken the Vladivostok terms and said, "Let's call this a treaty," essentially deferring all of the controversial points which we could not agree upon. The alternative was a comprehensive proposal which involved such extensive cuts in weapons systems and in the ability to improve qualitative capabilities on both sides that it came as rather a surprise to the Soviet government, and in fairly short order, the U.S. delegation was advised that this was not acceptable. Two months later another meeting was arranged, with Secretary of State Vance and Foreign Minister Gromyko conferring in Geneva in May, 1977, and agreeing on a framework for a SALT II Treaty controlling strategic offensive arms.

The agreement was to be in three parts. A basic treaty would last through 1985, setting overall ceilings and then providing for reductions—not very large ones, to be sure, but a good start for strategic nuclear disarmament. The ceilings were to be as high as at Vladivostok, 2,400 weapons systems on each side, but there were to be reductions to 2,250 systems (about a 10 percent reduction) during the life of that treaty. There were also subceilings on weapons with MIRVs, and some shorter-term limitations agreed to in principle—a protocol lasting three years—to cover those weapons systems which neither side had decided how to deal with over the longer period of time. And a third part of that three-part package would be a statement of principles governing SALT III, because integral to SALT is commitment to the idea that SALT is very much a continuing process.

In SALT II, we hope to put the brakes on and perhaps bring this vehicle called the arms race to a halt. Then, in successive courses of this many-course dinner, we can start to reduce the levels bit by bit. We must find new ways to apply qualitative controls, so that we do not just trade a halt on numerical buildup for expansion of some kind of technological leap forward in another direction—which has, unhappily, characterized so many of our early efforts at strategic arms control.

Rabbi Balfour Brickner, Professor James Forbes, Dr. Benjamin Spock, and Edith Lerrigo present Calls to Peace in the liturgy.

SALT II is now about 95 percent complete. It is an enormously complex technical document, sixty pages long, and full of all sorts of intricate details, prohibitions, limitations, ground rules for verification, and so forth, which are intended to insure that both sides will see this agreement as completely equitable, unambiguous, totally verifiable, and having within it the seeds of real reductions in SALT III and subsequent negotiations.

But it all seems to take so long and show so few results. After all, it has been eleven years since Glassboro; nine years since SALT negotiations began; over six years since SALT I was signed, and with it the interim agreement that was supposed to have been replaced by a treaty long before its expiration in October, 1977. Why does this process take so long to accomplish? Obviously, one answer is that controlling arms is essentially an unnatural thing for governments to do. Governments do not readily decide to jump up and limit their own arms or their own options in order to get some limitations on the other side. Instead we tend to say, "Well, we know how to build this weapon, and maybe the other side will build it, too; but if we get the jump on them, maybe we will be better off."

Relations with the Soviet Union

Furthermore, there is a deep-seated uneasiness in this country about negotiating with the Soviet Union, partly because of disenchantment with the idea of détente, which I think many people feel was somewhat oversold back in the 1972–1973 period when President Nixon went to Moscow and increasingly began to use his foreign policy successes to bolster his rapidly eroding support at home. Another reason for the uneasiness has been a steady barrage of propaganda, largely from unofficial sources, but occasionally even from official sources, all aimed at scaring the American people about Soviet intentions and capabilities, and downgrading our own strengths and capabilities—not only the military capabilities but also the essential strengths of the American economic and social structure.

What we have today, widespread around this country, is essentially a paradox. People are tired of the arms race and of spending money on nuclear weapons. When polls are taken, 70-75 percent of the public says, "We want a SALT agreement, and we want it fast." But then you ask, "How do you feel about a SALT agreement with the Russians?" This time, 70 percent or more respond in the opinion polls, "We don't trust the Russians." So the question is: How do you deal with these paradoxical twin fears? How do you persuade people that we need an agreement; it is in our best interests; it is in their best interests too; and it is in the world's best interests to bring about this sort of agreement, because this is the only way to develop the kind of mutual relationships and eventual trust that will lead to better relations across the board?

I think we will be able to persuade the American people and the Congress that we *can* have it both ways. SALT is in their best interests, and although it is not everything they want, it has within it the seeds of something better. Furthermore, we are not negotiating out of trust, but out of our own self-interest, and the same is true on the part of the Soviet Union. SALT I and SALT II have shortcomings for everyone. Everyone has an ideal treaty, but no one is going to get it. The test of a good treaty should be: (1) Can it deter nuclear war? I think that SALT will. (2) Can it be achieved without exacting an unacceptable price? I would say "Yes" to that, too, and I think that our political leaders need to know that an unacceptable price need not be paid.

We have read reports and heard rumors—not all of them accurate—about various efforts to see if this or that vote can be bought, or if the military can be brought into camp with various programs. I was pleased to hear the president say at a recent press conference that we do not have a nuclear war-fighting strategy, that he never approved a $2 billion civil-defense program, that we have not decided to go ahead with the MX multiple-aim-point system or all those other gadgets which are supposed to make SALT easier for one or two pivotal senators to stomach.

The Need for Arms Control

SALT II, when completed, will be neither as good as it ought to be, nor as bad as some will inevitably say it is. Some critics, not waiting to see the final text, claim that it gives the Soviet Union great military advantages, undermines our allies, does not cope with the real threats—and we should not be dealing with "them" anyway, because of their human rights record, what they are doing with the Cubans in Africa, or whatever reason. Others are going to say that SALT does nothing about disarmament and that it only rationalizes and ratifies the arms race, and they are right. It is not going to accomplish disarmament as such, but it has in it the capacity to build toward a real disarmament approach. Still others will complain that too high a price is being paid; that a big civil defense program will be effected; that the MX multiple-aim-point (shell game) missile deployment systems will be pushed ahead; that the Trident Missile will be accelerated; and that a new nuclear war-fighting strategy will be adopted to go along with all this.

Let me recapitulate what the SALT treaty will and will not do. It will prevent further numerical escalation of strategic offensive weapons. It will stop the buildup, actually at a point where U.S. forces are slightly below Soviet forces; so it will require the Soviet Union to dismantle and destroy some of its weapons. It will limit, in some respects, the qualitative arms race in strategic weapons—for example, the so-called "fractionation," or the number of warheads that can be put on missiles. When I said that the United States has nine thousand nuclear weapons and the Soviet Union nearly five thousand, that is, of course, by multiplying the warheads sitting atop a smaller number of actual missiles. We have reached agreement in principle to limit the number of warheads that will go on these weapons, and although it will still be a very high number, it will be much less than it would have been without these limits.

SALT will indeed preserve some military options. It will not require us or the Soviets to exercise those options, but again, such decisions have to be made on the basis of considerations other than arms control. Whether we have the wisdom *not* to exercise them is very much a result of whether we can exercise the political will to restrain ourselves, whether we can see that it may be in our best interests not to go ahead on some possible programs. This is where the protocol element of SALT is really an asset. It controls such weapons as cruise missiles and mobile missiles (both ground-launched and air-launched). It says in effect, "Think over the implications of going ahead with some of these weapons."

There is always enormous pressure to go ahead with all of these weapons just because it can be done. But that is not sufficient justification to launch ourselves headlong, blindfolded into a world where suddenly we have to cope, for example, with both sides having tens of thousands of ground-launched cruise missiles—nuclear and non-nuclear—perhaps all over Central Europe. Is it in our interest to do that, just because we have the capability right now? We have to think that through. We had this experience with MIRVs back in 1969–1970. We learned how to multiply the killing power of strategic missiles many times over by putting little warheads on them that could go off in different directions after the missiles were launched, so that they could attack and destroy numerous targets many hundreds of miles apart.

We considered the MIRVs such wonderful gimmicks that we hardly thought for a minute of controlling our appetite for building them. Now we are haunted by the specter of a scenario, albeit bizarre, where the Soviet Union, with its MIRV warheads—which they went ahead and developed very effectively—could theoretically threaten the survival of our land-based missile silos. This would never have happened if we had instead decided to agree to halt the MIRV race before it even began. We could have agreed to a ban on testing them in the first place. In 1974, Dr. Kissinger was asked at a press conference if he felt that we should have gone ahead with MIRV, and he said he wished we had thought through the implications more carefully before we went ahead with the MIRV testing programs. The same can apply to cruise missiles, multiple-basing systems for the Minuteman, MX, or any other kind of land-based missile.

SALT II will also promote our nonproliferation objectives. It is not that countries are necessarily waiting to decide about signing the nonproliferation treaty pending our decision on signing SALT II. But if we fail to conclude a SALT agreement, it will be a signal to the rest of the world that we are not serious about our commitment to arms control, and they will be more inclined to go ahead with their own nuclear weapons.

SALT II will not stop all weapons programs, nor will it guarantee détente. The political forces behind the military competition are likely to continue; we cannot resolve all our differences through SALT or any other arms control program. But I think that SALT II will insure stability, improve security, and provide a hope for future disarmament. Therefore, it deserves and will get the support of both the people and Congress.

Finally, what is the alternative to a SALT agreement? We can count on endless escalation costing hundreds of billions of dollars—all to wind up no better than we were before. The nature of the new weapons coming along is such that there will be more and more temptation for military commanders and political leaders to use them in times of crisis, where today they might be deterred. Détente, such as it is, will collapse entirely, resulting in a decrease in security everywhere. The likelihood of nuclear proliferation around the world will be greatly increased, so that the chances of a nuclear conflagration in which there will be no winners will increase enormously. SALT provides an alternative to that dread prospect, and I think we should seize that alternative.

DÉTENTE AND DISARMAMENT—U.S.S.R.

Yuri S. Kapralov

In my view, this conference is a very significant event, because it is a vivid manifestation of a growing understanding on the part of the general public in the United States of the necessity to bring an end to the arms race, and to bring about concrete, definite measures for arms control and disarmament. We in the Soviet Union welcome the broad movement in favor of peace and disarmament, because we consider disarmament to be the very central means of insuring the peace and the security of all nations.

What is our stand on this issue? We are in favor of universal and complete disarmament. We consider this task to be not only desirable, not only urgent, but also feasible. We believe that there are necessary prerequisites and very strong incentives for disarmament for different countries with different social and political structures. We also believe that the general public has a major role to play in the process of easing international tensions and promoting disarmament. For us in the Soviet Union, disarmament is not a slogan, and it is not a policy of the moment. The struggle for disarmament has its history, its continuity, and its reasons.

Soviet Peace Efforts

It is symbolic that the first legislative act of the Soviet state was a decree on peace. This decree was issued on the second day of our

YURI S. KAPRALOV is First Secretary, Soviet Embassy, Washington, D.C., specializing in arms control and disarmament. He formerly held the U.S. Desk, Soviet Foreign Ministry, Moscow.

existence back in 1917, and in this decree the Soviet government made an appeal to all nations—to all governments—to stop the war that was raging throughout the world at that time. We appealed to nations to disband armies and to make peace. It is equally symbolic that sixty years later, in Article 28 of our new Constitution which was adopted only a year ago, the task of universal and complete disarmament was set forth as a major, practical goal of Soviet foreign policy.

Why is it that the Soviet Union is pushing so strongly in favor of peace and in favor of disarmament? There are some very substantial reasons. For one thing, in the sixty years of our existence, approximately one-half of that period was taken away by wars and by periods of reconstruction, or periods when we tried to restore the economy and tried to make up for losses—if we can ever make up for losses of human beings. During the last war alone—which is known to the world as the Second World War, and which is known to most Soviet people as the Great Patriotic War because it was the war for survival of my country—we lost more than twenty million people. They were men, women, and children. We also had about seventy thousand villages and approximately seventeen hundred cities and towns destroyed. So we know by firsthand experience what war means, especially modern war. That is why we in the Soviet Union are determined not to let it happen again. (Just as a matter of reference, I would mention that the United States lost about 500,000 servicemen during those tragic days; less than the number of people who died in auto accidents in the United States during that period.)

Equally fundamental and significant is the fact that in my country, in our sociopolitical system as well as in our ideology, we reject war as a means of settling international disputes. The Soviet society, by its nature, is oriented toward internal development, toward raising the living standards of our people, and toward satisfying their needs. Contrary to the situation in some other countries, we do not have any political or social class, or any social group with an inherent interest in military production or in pursuing the arms race. It is also important to note that in our country, we have enough of all kinds of resources not to have to look to other countries. So war just does not make sense for us. Except in self-defense, war will serve no practical purpose whatsoever. So, when you are sometimes told that there is a Soviet threat to you, to the United States, you should know that it is simply a big lie which is designed either to justify growing military spending or somebody's political or personal ambitions.

To sum up, we need peace to continue our internal development, our internal construction. We are not going to attack anybody. At the same time, in view of the lessons of the past, we cannot afford unilateral disarmament. In this connection, the question arises: Would the United States benefit from disarmament? In my mind there is only one answer: Yes, positively. The United States would benefit immensely from disarmament, both in terms of national security and in terms of economic development. I mention economic development because, at least according to our theory, military expenditures constitute nothing but great burdens for any kind of economic system, whether it is socialist, capitalist, or anything else. I believe that here, military spending is a major factor of inflation—and you know that better than I do.

The Need for Disarmament

I also mentioned national security interests because military experts here, both within the administration and outside, are often talking about whether one or another agreement will strengthen the national security of the United States. I would just suggest that we remember old days—for instance, the years before the Second World War. Just to make a very simple comparison, before the Second World War, the United States had rather small armed forces. At that time, as far as I know, we had ten times more armed forces than you had. Yet, at that time there was no talk—in terms of today's language—about the Soviet threat or the Russians coming.

Then the United States built an atomic bomb and dropped it on Japan, and that changed the situation in the world. After that, the United States introduced strategic bombers and more strategic bombers, then intercontinental ballistic missiles, then took those ballistic missiles to submarines, then equipped those missiles with multiple independently targetable reentry vehicles, then introduced or designed the cruise missile. And the latest programs are very destabilizing. So now you have very great military might. But do you feel safer? I think we all know—at least you talk about it—that you do not feel safer. I think that as simplistic as it may be, this comparison at least gives us an idea that nobody can win the arms race. And nobody will feel safer if it continues.

We consider disarmament, as I said, to be urgent, desirable, and also feasible. It is a task that we, together with other countries, can accomplish. Since the Second World War, the Soviet Union has introduced, proposed, or put forward about one hundred proposals aimed at curbing and eventually halting the arms race, reducing military spending, and preventing the development of new systems of weapons for mass annihilation. It is, to a great extent, due to our efforts (and I am proud of it) that the world at large began more and more to realize the danger of the arms race and the necessity of stopping it—of reversing the arms race. As you know, the U.N. Special Session on Disarmament took place in this city last May. At that session, the Soviet Union put forward a comprehensive program on practical ways to curb the arms race. We do not claim that we have all the instant, exhaustive answers to all questions arising from such a complex problem, but we are prepared to consider any constructive, sensible proposal, and to this end, we believe that this program which we introduced is a balanced, reasonable basis for the job to be done.

Where do we stand now? What is the status of this problem of disarmament? As I said, the Soviet Union is in favor of universal and complete disarmament. But I think it is clear that with all the burdens of the past, it cannot be achieved within a fortnight, and I think we all realize that. There should be—and there are—some measures which can be taken now in order to promote the cause of disarmament. We believe that the immediate task for both the Soviet Union and the United States is to accomplish, without delay, agreements on subjects under discussion. The most important, of course, is the SALT agreement.

SALT

As we see it, the SALT agreement would not only stabilize the existing situation—I mean the situation of rough equivalents, or rough parity—and not only put quantitative and, for the first time, qualitative restrictions on the most deadly systems; but this agreement would also contribute to the improvement of political relations. This is very important, but I think it is often overlooked here in the United States, because people tend to talk in terms of numbers or specific theories. They just overlook the fact that such an agreement, which is connected with the feeling of security, would immensely contribute to better political relations between our countries. I think it would create a favorable atmosphere for bringing to a successful conclusion other talks and discussions on arms control and disarmament. The effect of the SALT agreement would be even greater if coupled with another agreement on the Comprehensive Test Ban Treaty which is now being negotiated between the Soviet Union and the United States, with the participation of the United Kingdom.

In short, what is needed now is a breakthrough which would reverse the present trend toward increasing deadly weapons, both in numbers and in quality. In my view, the early accomplishment of the SALT agreement and maybe the Comprehensive Test Ban Treaty and other agreements would represent a starting point in the present situation for reversing the arms race; it would start that process again of the betterment of our relations, trying to reduce further the danger of war.

And what is the role of the general public in this process? I think the role of the general public in the political process is increasing, especially now. I think the general public can generate political will which sometimes some governments lack; and since this disarmament program is intended to educate people and to prepare people to struggle for this very just cause of peace and disarmament, I would like to wish this program, its leaders, and all of you every success in this noble endeavor.

THEOLOGICAL IMPLICATIONS OF THE ARMS RACE

Robert McAfee Brown

This is not a "How-To" lecture: "How to Organize Your Community," "How to Get Carter to Change His Mind," "How to Levitate the Pentagon," or even "How to Love the Bomb." Other parts of this conference deal with strategies and tactics, so this is not a "Next-Steps" lecture either. It is simply an attempt to *begin* some reflection on aspects of the arms race in the light of our faith. I speak as a Christian, although I want to be sensitive to the concerns of Jews as well.

With what kinds of theological resources do we confront this dizzying spectacle of arms escalating to increasingly insane proportions? With what kinds of resources do we move on to the "next step" or "how to" questions?

I start with a theological quotation from an anonymous seventeenth-century writer: "I had rather see coming toward me a whole regiment with drawn swords, than one lone Calvinist convinced that he is doing the will of God."

That comment illustrates both the greatness and the demonic quality of Calvinism, and by extension, all other theological positions. (To paraphrase Karl Rahner, we are all "anonymous Calvinists.") Calvinism is demonic because it is far too easy for people to determine what *they* want to do and then decide that it is also the will of God. No bad idea can be anything but worse when divine

ROBERT McAFEE BROWN is Professor of Ecumenics and World Christianity, Union Theological Seminary, New York City.

sanction is claimed for it. This is the "Kill-a-Commie-for-Christ" syndrome that is far more deeply ingrained in our culture than we would care to admit. For the sake of "Christian civilization," and in opposition to that tautological opponent, "atheistic godless Communism," we can bring ourselves to do the most demonic things—such as building thirty thousand nuclear weapons—and call it the doing of God's will. Clearly, there is a demonization.

But there is also a glory in the statement. Calvinists have been marvelously freed by the thought that perhaps, in acting, they were doing God's will. If I feel that it is God's will for me to do x, I can be liberated from fear of failing or from lacking courage to take risks; freed to attempt what otherwise I might not attempt, since I can count on the ultimate disposition of what I do coming from God. It may be my lot to fail, so that someone else can learn from my failure; or it may be that I will do more than I might otherwise have attempted, because I believe that I am not alone and that God empowers me in the doing of what needs to be done.

Needless to say, it is the second of these attitudes rather than the first that I commend. We face immense problems, seemingly insuperable barriers, and overwhelming odds in even thinking about reversing the arms race. So powerful are the forces arrayed against us, that one is almost tempted to throw in the towel before beginning. But if we can believe that it is the will of God for God's children to live in peace, rather than to die in war—a proposition which is not particularly difficult for me to entertain—then perhaps we can be energized into seeing ourselves as instruments for carrying out that will. And if we can so see ourselves, there are new heights to which we might conceivably rise. The odds are mammoth, but we can declare ourselves with a little more abandon and courage if we believe that the divine intention is being fulfilled as we work for a reversal of the arms race instead of an escalation of it. I am willing to gamble that this is so. Join me.

Within that overall framework, I offer seven considerations for you to reflect upon.

1. Let us consider how we think theologically about the arms race.

I confess that I have been going through a Copernican revolution. Not too many years ago, I would have taken about half a dozen doctrines—God, Christ, church, human nature, sin, salvation, and so on—spelled them out briefly as "timeless truths," and then sought to "apply" them to the matter at hand—in this case the arms race, although the application could have been to alcoholism, sex, or racism, depending on the occasion. But I have become disenchanted with that approach.

For one thing, I do not think the gospel consists of "timeless truths" that exist in some kind of vacuum just waiting to be applied. I think our theologies grow out of the situations in which we find ourselves. They are forged as we act, wrestle, contend, fear, fail, and sometimes even win modest victories. As Gutiérrez said, theology is "the second act," while commitment is the first. Theology is "critical reflection on praxis," as we bring our critical faculties into play, in the light of a gospel that also came out of conflict situations. So I want to start with the situation and see what kind of theological conclusions it forces on us.

Think about this: How does one describe our human situation in terms of the arms race? The answer is very simple: madness and sheer insanity. In the name of trying to be "realistic," we have lost touch with reality. We can kill everybody in the world twelve times; so we want to increase that killing capacity to perhaps fifteen or sixteen times. We have thirty thousand nuclear weapons in our stockpile, and Russia has at least half that many; yet we nod without quibbling when military men, whose way of life depends on it, tell us that we need still more. We talk about building more weapons to make our situation safer, when each weapon we build actually makes our situation more precarious. We talk about the death of 140 million people in a preemptive first strike as an "acceptable" loss of life.

One need not elaborate on the script. The possibilities for irony, satire, or tragedy are legion. There is no logic to it. It is simply and utterly mad, particularly reduced to one proposition: The more weapons we build, the less secure we are; therefore we will build more weapons! This is madness, in the sense of being utterly out of touch with reality, unable to discern what is going on, unable to read the signs of the times—a kind of madness we could call "clinical madness." People who think this way (even more, people who *act* this way) should be "certifiable." They should be locked up to protect the world from them. But they are the ones who run the Pentagon, the Congress, the multinationals, and the White House. There is a bit of this madness in every one of us whenever we start the argument from a narrowly defined view of "national security." So our new theological starting point is the madness—the insanity of the world around us.

2. How does the gospel propose to deal with this madness?

One might propose that we pit sanity against madness—if we could figure out what sanity was. Let me offer a counterproposal: Against the clinical madness of the people who are running things and making the decisions, we need what Abraham Heschel called "moral madness"—the madness of the prophets.

The prophets refused to accept the state of things around them as normative. They proposed new allegiances, fresh ways of looking at life, challenges to those in authority. They were very angular: Amos never even won third prize in the "Bethel Chamber of Commerce Annual Award for Promising Young Dressers of Sycamore Trees"; Jeremiah wasn't ever asked back to preach a second time after his candidating sermon. On at least four occasions in the Hebrew Scriptures, the prophets are described as "mad," meaning quite simply that *they did not conform to the norms of their society.*

Without taking on too many prophetic mantles too pretentiously, let us at least affirm that a basic theological task of our time, in relation to the arms race, is a similar one: to refuse to conform to the norms of *our* society. Let us begin with the premise that the people running things have got it all wrong; their priorities are skewed, their visions of the future are incorrect; their remedies are no remedies at all but rather recipes for disaster. Let us determine that we are not going to buy into a way of looking at the future that says, "The more precarious we make it, the better it will be for everybody." Let us have the brashness to affirm that whatever we know or do not know about God's will, we do know at least that having created this earth, God is not now urging earth's children to destroy it, or at least to destroy one another.

Against the clinical madness of the Pentagon mentality, let us at least try to pose the moral madness of a prophetic tradition that challenges the principalities and powers of this world; a moral madness that claims to be answerable to someone or something else, however hard it may be to get absolutely clear directions. At the very least, we know that some directions are wrong, and that whatever the direction is to be, it will be different from the one to which the so-called "wise" men of our time seek to point us. Let us opt for moral madness.

3. **Part of the clinical madness is that human community is either denied or defined in such restrictive terms that it excludes almost every other community besides our own.**

We are willing to destroy other communities, such as the Russian or Chinese, to "save" our own, even though an attempt to destroy them will almost inevitably mean the destruction of much of our own

Robert McAfee Brown, theologian from Union Theological Seminary, addressing a breakfast meeting of the convocation.

community. In such situations, it is a travesty to talk about "community." We can talk about competing forces, ideological opponents, or whatever, but we cannot really talk about community.

What would be an appropriate response to the sort of human expression of madness that says we have to destroy community in order to save it (which is nothing more than Ben Tre in Vietnam writ large)? To me, the response is increasingly clear: A global community is the only possible alternative, and I have discovered that we do not need to create this global community since it already exists. It exists for me in the Christian church, or rather in a *remnant* of the Christian church, which says, "We will define who we are, not first as Americans, or white, or rich, or middle class, but as members of the global family." Jews, making the necessary translations, can do the same thing.

If the crying need is for a sense of global community, we can engage in at least modest rejoicing, for that community is already around. It surfaces every now and then when people rally against a racist assault or against a barbarous war in Southeast Asia; when Beyers Naudé or Steve Biko say "no" to the South African government; when Helder Camara stands against military tyranny in the northeast of Brazil. *We are not, even now, alone.* We are part of a cloud of witnesses, a communion of saints. And let us not ever forget it. When you feel alone, or weak, or lacking courage, remember: We have a model we can live out; a "preview of coming attractions" (which is one of my favorite definitions of the church these days), in which people might see enough of that coming attraction—however fractured by sin—to want to become part of such a community. Don't ever undersell what that means for us now, and for others in the future.

4. As we look at the horrors around us, we have to rethink our understanding of the human person—what in our more chauvinistic past we called "the doctrine of man."

What does the present situation say about who we really are? Our society seems to be made up of people who are fearful; so fearful that they have surrendered to a concept of "national security" that purports to assuage that fear, but at the cost of turning their power and decision-making authority over to others. But over to whom? Who are the ones we really trust?

Basically, we trust the military people who love the bomb, produce the charts at Senate hearings, have the "hard sell"—"do what we say or the Russians will destroy us"—and wrap their authority in a uniformed aura that makes it well-nigh unchallengeable. We let the military people make the decisions that control our domestic and foreign policy. The old-fashioned way was just the reverse. Our domestic and foreign-policy decisions determined what military postures we took. I liked it better the old-fashioned way.

Now, we not only trust the military mind, we and they place our final trust in computers. The computers will decide whether or not a nuclear war will start. The human factor is increasingly ruled out, and military minds are formed by what the computer feeds into them. Again, the old-fashioned way was to have the computers informed by the information *we* fed into them. I liked it better the old-fashioned way here, too. We have surrendered our ability to control our own destiny. We have turned it over to generals and admirals, who in turn

salute the Chief of Staff, who turns out to be a box with the letters
"I.B.M." written across its chest.

What a view of human nature! What a betrayal! We need to work
theologically to find a counterview. What I have been describing is
what the Bible calls idolatry, giving absolute allegiance to that which
merits only conditional allegiance, whether it is a man with gold braid
on his sleeve, or a box with printouts disgorging from its belly. To
these we must bow the knee? To these we must say "Almighty"? To
these we must surrender our freedom and our capacity for decision
making?

What is called for here is the beginning of *nay-saying;* of
challenging the power of such authorities; of acknowledging that any
God worthy of the name and worthy of allegiance will not be the God
of *one* nation or race or class, but of all. The sooner we begin to
explore ways to topple the idols and return our allegiance to the
proper source, the better the prospect for human survival.

To serve the Pentagon or the computer—assuming that there is a
difference—is not to have achieved freedom; it is to have attained the
ultimate in bondage, since it is finally an allegiance that leads to
death. To serve the God of Abraham and Isaac, of Sarah and Leah,
and the God of Jesus Christ is, in a paradoxical way, to find freedom
rather than bondage; to be free to opt for life instead of death, for
choice instead of puppetry, for a future instead of only a past with
nobody around even to take note of it. Put another way, this means a
new set of priorities. Remember the neutron bomb that destroys
people but not buildings. *Things* become ultimate. We will have a
"safe" world if it kills us (which it will); so safe that nobody can hurt
anything any more because there won't be anybody around to *do*
anything—except buildings, and they are not very good at that.

5. **Let us expand our view of the human person by asking what the
situation tells us about the dark side of human nature—what
theologians call sin.**

Here we learn some menacing things. Sin seems not to be a
rebellion lodged in individuals: We are not on a collision course with
disaster because a few evil people are maneuvering us in that
direction. Rather we are on a collision course with disaster because all
the good people are impotent. The power has gone out of their hands,
not to evil people, but to a set of structures that virtually have a life of
their own which we can no longer control. Sin is systemic. Sin is not
just writ small in the human heart—though God knows there is
enough and more right there. It is writ large in the social structures

that surround and increasingly engulf us. There is a kind of technological inevitability in things. If something is bigger, it is better; and if it is better, we must have it; so if it can be built, we will build it. If we cannot make appropriate decisions in response to complex data, the computers will do it for us.

The decision makers in the Pentagon are not sitting around saying, "Let's see now, how can we disfigure babies; how can we burn elderly people; how can we mutilate the cream of our youth?" Yet their corporate actions lead inevitably in such directions. There is a power of evil abroad, so menacing and so threatening that we can hardly contemplate it. And this is not just true in relation to the possibility of nuclear war. It is true in relation to the fact that children today starve by the thousands, not because bad people will it, but because good decent people like us are accomplices in structures of corporate evil, and without wanting to do so, we are consenting to the starvings, the burnings, the mutilations.

If the sin is somehow lodged in the structures, at least part of the remedy will have to be redemption of those structures, which may well mean their overthrow—and nobody likes to hear that kind of talk, particularly parishioners on Sunday morning, most of whom work night and day for those same structures, and without whose munificent profits most of us in ministry would not be making a living wage. We are as caught and dependent as anybody else, and just to realize *that* would be a large part of the battle in working to create some alternate structures.

Another part of the task would be to stop scapegoating; to realize that it is cheap evasion blaming it all on the Russians, or the Communists, or the Cubans, or the Chinese, or even (as I may have come perilously close to doing) the Pentagon, as though all responsibility could be placed in front of a single door. We will need a lot of know-how to talk about alternate structures, and we had better begin to acquire it. We could begin with the churches, making them the sort of alternative structures that could provide some new models and options for change.

6. **That is part of the human picture. Where does a theological perspective come in? Where do we find God in such a scenario?**

Theologically, we had better take much more seriously in our day what our forebears described as "divine judgment." I am not interested in resurrecting a view of a vengeful deity hurling thunderbolts at recalcitrants. I am very much interested in affirming that somehow, in the long run if not the short, this is a moral universe, and we can get away with evil for just so long, until there comes some kind of retribution, some kind of judgment. That is not the easiest thing to affirm these days; the Nazi holocaust makes it hard, not only to believe in a loving God, but also in a judging God. Where was God in those holocaust years when God was so badly needed? These equations are not easy, and they are even more complicated in relation to the arms race, because by the time judgment finally comes, it may be so devastatingly efficient that nobody will escape and be around to notice it and profit from the lesson.

At least we can affirm a kind of ghastly logic that seems to be vindicated in our increasing reliance on arms to save us: *The more dependent we become on arms, the less secure we are.* The ratio is inverse. Perhaps that is a secular statement about the judgment of God. To put ultimate reliance in the wrong thing is to have all reliances threatened; to trust the wrong God is to have mistrust take over everything. To let loose atomic wastes is to guarantee cellular destruction in our grandchildren, should they live so long. There is at least a negative moral logic at work in this situation, but you won't escape it by looking elsewhere and giving it a different name. The reality with which we have to conjure is this: *You may think you are getting away with it, but you are not.* Let that be a rather basic lesson for our culture.

7. That is quite a bit of denunciation. Remember that Paolo Freire says there must not be only denunciation, but also annunciation.

There is not only darkness but at least some light, or we would not know we were in the dark. Here and there people spring up with new visions. We should indulge in some vision-tasting. We should look for signs indicating that people are in protest against the Pentagon mentality and join forces with them. We should exalt every word or deed suggesting that the human family is more important than just the American family, or that the white family is not worth preserving at the expense of the black family. We should be that group of people who will announce alternatives—who will use the word "conversion" not only to talk about changes in one's soul, but also about job conversion, factory conversion, energy conversion, all kinds of conversion. There is plenty of expertise to accomplish such concerns in our culture.

To say this is not to substitute some humanistic scheme that has been drained of all theological content. Don't let anybody pull that line on you! This is saying, "Whatever else the kingdom of God may be, it is a reality in which people dwell together in peace because there is justice." It is saying, "Wherever else the kingdom of God may be, it must be here on earth, and our job is to be instruments through which its creation can be manifested more fully." It is saying, "Whoever else Jesus Christ may be, he is one who lives among us, sides with the poor and destitute, and affirms their worth at whatever cost to himself." It is saying, "There are tasks to be done here and now, and they can be tried here and now."

We do not need "one lone Calvinist" anymore; we do need lots and lots of people who will say: "I've only got a piece of the vision, but I'll work with what I've got." We need people who will say: "I've not been all the way up to the mountaintop with Brother Martin, but I've seen far enough to realize that things don't need to be the way they are." We need people who will say: "We may not know all the right directions, but we surely know some of the wrong ones, and we can say good-bye to them." We need people who will say: "At least we've got to examine socialism and not let it be the 'scare-word' of the generation; at least we've got to challenge capitalism and not let it be the sacrosanct word of the generation; at least we've got to investigate some new mixes of the two that don't escalate into Stalinism, but also don't escalate into the mind-blowing profits that are clutched by the few at the cost of hope, and even life, to the many."

* * * * *

All of which brings me to a conclusion. We have already noted that Christians are in the season of Advent. I do not say that to exclude Jews, although I will stick with the Advent imagery since there is a part of it that Jews can affirm as well.

Advent is a time of waiting: There is a rumor around that things might get better, that somebody might come and give us help in making them better. There are wisps of hope here and there. Somebody is coming. What will he be like? Who knows for sure? We have welcomed him many times, but he wears different garb in different ages. We cannot be sure. Who we wait for may not be who comes. What our society wants vindicated may be challenged. In a war-bent world, who can really welcome one known as the Prince of Peace? In a society that brutally oppresses millions of its own members, who can welcome a Liberator who talks about freeing the captives and bringing liberty to the oppressed? In a time when power is the name of the game, who is going to look twice at the epitome of sheer powerlessness—a baby?

Through all this, what the Advent season says is, *"Be ready for surprises."* The one who comes may be totally other than you anticipate. You want a sense of mystery in which it is appropriate to "let all mortal flesh keep silence"? Very well; but perhaps he will come in such a way that the very stones will cry out if you do not. You want a gentle Savior? Very well; but perhaps he will come in a different guise, as one of the Advent hymns points out:

> He comes to break oppression, To set the captives free,
> To take away transgression, And rule in equity.
> He comes with succor speedy. To those who suffer wrong,
> To help the poor and needy, And bid the weak be strong.

Nobody knows how he will come this time, so once again, be ready for surprises. That means we can look ahead with hope. It means that we are not locked into a situation devoid of the possibility of change. It means that "more of the same" can never be the last word, and that we get the shock of our lives when the Advent is fulfilled. It means that despair is toppled from top billing. It means that things can be different. It means that we can be energized into taking on even the toughest job of our time—reversing the arms race—not because we have all the expertise (though we need all we can get); not because we have the most numbers (though the more like-minded people we can gather, the better our case will be); not because victory is sure (though we must live as though it were, and at the same time work like hell to make it so—which I offer as a modern definition of the theological doctrine of sanctification).

We can run with perseverance the race that is set before us; we can rejoice in the cloud of witnesses; we can avoid succumbing to despair, because we are convinced that in our universe there is something with which we can side, which also works for peace and justice rather than war and destruction. (If we are Jews, we can look for a first coming, if Christians, for a second; but we can look together because all that really separates us at this point is that we have different timetables.)

We can find staying power, not because we generate it out of our own juices, but because deep in our heart of hearts, we are convinced that decency and hope and fresh beginnings have an eternal grounding, and that to be working for their realization is to be doing the work that is most noble, most fulfilling, and most bound to strike a responsive chord in other hearts as well.

ARMS RACE—
ECONOMIC DRAIN

Seymour Melman

The role of the United States in the worldwide arms race is sustained, not only by a powerful industrial economic base, but also by the prevalence of a system of illusion which obscures the nature of critical realities.

Thus, it is widely believed that the way in which the Second World War ended the Great Depression can be a model for a sustaining economy—an illusion. The American experience in the Second World War lasted four years, but the present arms race has been going on for more than thirty. The four-year experience in World War II involved enlarging the labor force by more than eleven million people from among the unemployed and counting on the capital goods of the country to endure through four years of heavy use. They did endure. The buildings, homes, railroads, power plants, and factories could all endure four years of use, but they have not been able to endure thirty years of neglect. The decay resulting from a thirty-year arms race is evident on the streets of New York City—breakdowns in the water supply, failure of the sanitation service, poor public transportation, and the physical rot of urban housing.

Failure to replace productive plants and equipment has made incompetence epidemic in American industry. Since 1965, the United States has had the lowest rate of productivity growth of any industrial country in the world. Further, the widely cherished belief that the

SEYMOUR MELMAN is Professor of Industrial Engineering, Columbia University; cochairman, SANE; and author of *The Permanent War Economy; Pentagon Capitalism;* and *Our Depleted Society.*

United States is first in industrial technology is now false. Whereas we were once the highest-wage-paying country in the world, we now rank fifth, with countries that have had less participation in the arms race ranking first.

The illusion prevails that the war economy creates wealth simply because money changes hands for work done.[1] But the outcome of work done on behalf of the military system yields nothing that can be used either in current consumption or for future production.[1] However intricate a Polaris Submarine, an ICBM, and a modern war plane, they have no economic value in the ordinary sense of the term.

The Unwinnable Arms Race

Believing that the arms race can be won by superior military power is a widely held illusion. We have long since passed the point where anyone knows how to define military superiority. That point was passed when nuclear weapons became abundant in a number of countries. Therefore, the arms race is a race which all sides must lose. Even the term "arms race" contains illusion, because in other kinds of races—the athletic sort—there is a winner and a loser, and that has colored our understanding of the term. But that ordinary expectation of the presence of a winner is false with respect to the arms race.

According to the best available knowledge, a major nuclear exchange would, among other things, weaken the ozone layer around the earth, permitting ultraviolet radiation of such intensity that it would destroy crops and induce cancer on a mass scale among the humans remaining. This was explained by Philip Handler, president of the National Academy of Sciences, in a November 26, 1975, Op-Ed piece in the *New York Times,* but it seems to have been forgotten. It is treated as a "1984" fact to be put into a memory bank and otherwise ignored. There is no conceivable technical way of emerging unscathed from a so-called "totally successful" first strike, because the backlash from the destruction of the ozone layer around the earth will reach the very country that launches the successful first strike. In Handler's words, there is "no escape." The arms race cannot possibly be won.

It is also an illusion to suppose that the United States is heading in the direction of success by developing a better airplane, a better cannon, a better artillery shell, a better missile, a better Band-Aid, a better foodpack. The assumption that the accumulation of particular technical gains yields an aggregate military superiority is flawed. It is based on the false assumption that military power applied in the aggregate can yield a winner on the one hand and a definable loser on the other. But in this era of mass availability of nuclear weapons, that prospect is checkmated.

We tend to assume that a military firm is like any other—just another corporation. But this is not true. Military-industrial firms do not minimize cost to maximize profit, they maximize cost, aided by a maximization of subsidy received from the Department of Defense.

The assumption has been made that the United States is so rich that it can have guns *and* butter. This is also untrue. There is a finite quantity of resources, even in the U.S.A. There are only so many engineers, so many scientists, so many skilled workers, and those that are deployed for military work are not available for the rest.

Another illusion is that technology and productivity across-the-board are enhanced by a war economy. Wrong again. The most dramatic productivity growth of the last quarter of a century has been in precisely those countries with the lowest levels of participation in a military economy. Indeed, in the United States, the traceable consequence of giving massive priority in capital and technology to the military economy has been to downgrade the level of U.S. industrial technology and the rate of productivity growth.

There is one final illusion about the war economy which, in a way, is the last line of defense—the overarching illusion. While the people of this country are, in the ordinary sense, a religious people, there is also a secular religion that accompanies all others and often displaces them. The United States is committed to the worship of a God-state that is American nationalism. In the worship of that God-state, and in the assumption of its superiority, the high priest of that cult is the president of the United States, and the idol of that worship is the flag. If you want proof, just ask yourself whether the sight of the flag coming by simply inspires joy and good feeling, or is it reverence? Aren't we really encouraging the feeling of reverence by saluting the flag and pledging oaths to it—to a thing? Moses was right in warning against idol worship.

The idea of the God-state as all-powerful is a main underpinning of the system of illusion supporting the arms race. The idea that the God-state must not be weak helps to fuel support for the ever-growing military budget. The idea that the God-state must never be defeated helps to omit any reference to the Vietnam War from school curricula, even in the military academies, because the armed forces of the United States were defeated in Vietnam.

Problems in the Civilian Economy

Every economy has the task of organizing the community to work, because in order to live, a community must produce. A war economy has very special effects on that function because it preempts capital and technology, which are the crucial ingredients for production capability.

Since 1951, the yearly U.S. military budget has exceeded the net profits of all corporations. This means that the military budget, which is the equivalent of a capital fund because of its resources, is now *the* largest capital fund in the economy of the United States and has been for twenty-seven years. Moreover, the federal government dominates national spending for research and development, and 75–80 percent of the federal expenditures have been given over to the military during the last quarter of a century. The consequence has been to downgrade the efficiency of the civilian economy. U.S. labor productivity in the manufacturing industries used to grow at an average of 3–4 percent a year, but after 1965, it dropped to an average annual growth rate of 2.1 percent, and from 1970 to 1975, it fell even further to 1.8 percent—the lowest rate ever observed in the history of the United States, and the lowest growth rate of any industrial country in the world. This collapse of productivity growth has a controlling effect on present problems of inflation and unemployment, and the connection is crucial as an instrument in waging the campaign against the arms race.

Classically, American industrial firms used to offset cost increases, the better to minimize cost and maximize profit. Cost increases could be offset because there was productivity growth caused by investment in new machinery and new techniques in organization. But as the machinery-producing industries became less-competent designers and producers of new equipment, and as their output and skills were preempted for the military economy, there was a smaller supply of new, cost-attractive and competent machinery for U.S. manufacturing industries. What was available was both more intricate and more expensive, and therefore, it was not purchased as readily as before.

Since 1967, U.S. metal-working industries have had the oldest stock of metal-working machinery of any industrial country in the world. This decay has lowered productivity growth—the improvement of output-per-man-hour—so that manufacturers have been less able to offset cost increases by means of productivity growth. Being unable to offset cost increases, they swiftly learned that cost growth could be passed along to price, so cost-pass-along became the new microeconomy of U.S. industry. As it accelerated, price increases came at a rate that we call inflation—a rate so rapid as to cause a whole series of economic injuries, including reduction in the level of living and the purchasing power of money, with widespread effects.

As prices soared in the United States, producers abroad saw the opportunity to seize a piece of the American market. That is why half the shoes we wear are produced abroad, along with 20 percent of the cars we drive, all of the thirty-five-millimeter cameras, and the tuners and amplifiers for stereo sets. Wherever you turn—microphones, technical equipment, electron microscopes—sophisticated equipment and tools of all kinds are now imported. But importation means less work for Americans. Therefore, this has meant calamity for the unions of electrical workers, machinists, and steelworkers. It meant the closing down of the Youngstown, Ohio, steel plants—which is merely one incident in this parade of planned closings and loss of employment.

The consequences of economic depletion are visible in the condition of our cities whose physical decay is now everywhere.

Strategy for Change

In sum, the war economy is an anti-economy. It is destructive of the work opportunity and of the means of exchange—the currency which any society with a great division of labor has to use.

The strategy for an exit from the war economy is a political and economic strategy. We must relax the pressure from the five-million-person support system that is at the core of the military economy. We have to provide these people with a way out—the production workers, engineers, clerks, managers, and all the people in surrounding communities, such as hamburger-stand operators, real estate people, bankers, gas-station attendants. They have to see that there is an alternative to livelihood from the military economy. That is why we give priority at SANE to the strategy of preparing conversion planning from a military to a civilian economy.

There are five million persons directly engaged in the war economy, including the uniformed armed forces. But there are twelve states with so many persons dependent on the military that they constitute a swing vote. That is to say, when the war economy is an issue in those states, these people are numerous enough to give the majority vote to one or the other party. The concentration effect is very important, and it is amplified further by the fact that those twelve states together account for 30 percent of the total electoral vote in this country's national elections. To focus on conversion is therefore a strategic political and economic method for getting at the arms race.

There are a million civilians on the payroll of the DOD who

operate the arms race. There are from 150-175 people on the payroll of the Arms Control and Disarmament Agency to *regulate* the arms race. But there is not one single person employed by the U.S. government with the professional task of thinking about how to *reverse* the arms race. We will know that we are accomplishing our purpose when there is a national debate about conversion planning, and when nationwide pressure makes reversal of the arms race a top priority item for the government of the United States.

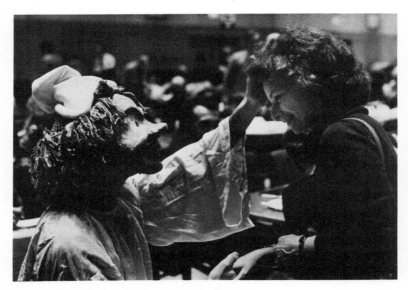

Ralph Lee's Giant Puppets lend spirit to the liturgy.

ARMS RACE—
THE NEED FOR CONVERSION

David Cortright

What do we mean by the whole concept of economic conversion? Actually, conversion is a different political approach to some basic questions. It is a way of reaching a much broader constituency and community than we have normally been able to reach. With a basic focus on the issue of job security, we can talk directly to the military-dependent workers and communities about their immediate employment security needs. And since we are really talking, not only about peace politics, but also about full-employment politics, this broadens the circle of people with whom we can communicate.

Our demands as peace activists are no longer simply "shut it down." It is no longer a case of getting rid of this or that military facility. Now we are going directly to the workers themselves in the communities and saying, "Let's talk about this. . . . Let's plan for alternatives. . . . Let's have a dialogue, keeping in mind our common interests, where our desire to reverse the arms race can intersect with your interest in a healthy, productive, civilian economy." This is what conversion is all about.

The Elements of Conversion

One of the most important things to consider in planning for

DAVID CORTRIGHT is Executive Director, SANE; co-founder, GI's United Against the War in Vietnam; and author of *Soldiers in Revolt— the American Military Today.*

conversion is a pre-notification system—an early warning system, if you will—so that a military base or a defense contractor can have some advance warning before a contract ends or a closing occurs. Then there will be time to plan. You do not simply learn the news on television that the president has just closed your industrial facility— as happened with the termination of the B-1 project. There was no advance warning and no possibility for any kind of realistic conversion plan. We do not want that kind of closing.

Another essential element of any conversion program is adjustment assistance, which is a fancy term for income support. During the transition period, from the time a facility is closed until alternative production can be brought in and the tools altered, there must be income support for the workers so that they are not victimized by the changeover and so that the community can maintain its overall living standard. We have had enough of the kind of situation where the workers become the scapegoats, bearing the basic burden of any change in Pentagon spending.

In the case of the B-1 project, Rockwell was not injured at all. In fact, it received more than $700 million to close down the facility. But several thousand production workers were simply thrown out. They had some unemployment insurance, but that quickly ran out, and they were placed in a very insecure position. We must have a program so that workers who are displaced because of reversal of the arms race or adjustments within the Pentagon budget have income security and retraining, as well as portability of their pensions, health-care systems, and all the other benefits which they have won through union contracts.

Another crucial element of conversion is a strong civilian-controlled economic adjustment office within the federal government. This agency should be able to assist local communities, unions, and workers in the process of converting to a civilian economy. But we do not need a massive block of buildings in Washington for this kind of effort. We need an agency which is competent in order to prepare guidelines and assist workers and communities in locating available facilities.

Still another cornerstone of conversion is alternative-use planning. There must be at every military facility—especially those facing imminent closure—a serious commitment to alternative-use planning, so that at Fort Dix, or Fort Sheridan, or at the B-1 facility, a plan is ready, earmarking those workers and facilities for a particular civilian activity. That way, the inventory of alternative uses will be available when the actual closing comes. But it is important that this planning be done on a decentralized basis. We do not want the agency in Washington planning what workers in the Southern California B-1 facility can do, because the people who know that facility best are the ones who work there. They have a sense of what the markets and the possibilities are in their area, and they are the ones who should have the responsibility and the authority to make decisions about what alternative uses will be brought into those facilities.

Finally, in terms of the ingredients of conversion, there must be a program of demand creation—an alternative agenda of public investment. It will do no good to have the most elaborate alternative-use plans on the shelves if there is no way to get some kind of commitment from industry or the federal government to purchase the products of these alternative uses. There are numerous such agendas available. In fact, one of the most elaborate was prepared at the end of the Vietnam War when President Johnson drew up a so-called "peace dividend" agenda, providing for billions of dollars of needed investment in social infrastructure production in the United States. And another innovative alternative agenda is about to be released by Gar Alperovitz's organization, The National Center for Economic Alternatives. It says that a federal commitment to purchases in four areas would more than make up for the lost demand and lost employment resulting from cutting back on the arms race. The four areas are: railroad rehabilitation, urban mass transit development, decentralized solar energy development, and biomass conversion (that is to say, conversion of wastes into synthetic gas). Work in these areas would do much to meet current problems.

A very exciting and encouraging development in this area during the last year has been the significant increase in participation and leadership from the trade union movement. There is dialogue and communication with labor that we have not had for a long time, and foremost in this coalition is the International Association of Machinists. Bill Winpisinger is truly a prophet in his views on the whole military economy, and he has been a strong advocate of conversion. So, too, has Doug Frazier, the new president of the United Auto Workers, who has made a commitment to reverse the arms race and to support the overall concept of conversion. And we have support from the Oil, Chemical, and Atomic Workers, the United Electrical Workers, some elements of the American Federation of Government Employees, and other major unions. They recognize the uncertainties of military employment, and because they are beginning to trust our sincere commitment to the jobs issue, they are willing to work with us.

The Government's Role

Conversion activity is moving forward rapidly, particularly in the areas of legislation, the new executive order, and local projects. One example of conversion legislation is the McGovern–Mathias Bill—The Defense Economic Adjustment Act. It was introduced last year by Senators George McGovern (D–S.D.) and Charles Mathias (R–Md.) for comments and initial support, and it will be reintroduced this year, hopefully with a large number of supporters. In the House, thirty-five representatives have cosponsored it.

This conversion planning bill would mandate committees of workers, management, and community people in every military facility to outline plans for alternative uses of these facilities. The important thing is that this legislation was developed in cooperation with labor. Last spring and summer, SANE and the offices of Senators McGovern and Mathias worked with representatives of various unions—Machinists; Auto Workers; Electricians; Oil; Chemical; and Atomic Workers; even with members of the AFL–CIO—so that this bill reflects the interests and concerns of all the trade unions.

Another important legislative vehicle is about to be introduced by Connecticut Congressman Chris Dodd, who comes from the southeastern part of the state where the Electric Boat facility is located, which probably makes him the most defense-dependent congressman in the whole House. But Dodd has recognized the vulnerability of his district to shifts in the military budget, and he has come forward as a strong advocate of conversion. Last summer, he convened a conference in Hartford that included the governor, several local congressmen and state representatives, as well as labor and industry officials, to talk about Connecticut's excessive dependence on the military. (One-quarter of the people in Connecticut work in defense production.) Soon, Congressman Dodd will be introducing legislation to encourage diversification and conversion.

Also significant is the new Carter executive order dealing with the question of military-base closings. Earlier this year, President Carter announced a "hit list" of bases to be closed—military facilities that have become redundant as the armed forces have shifted more and more to the south—including Fort Sheridan in Illinois, Fort Dix in New Jersey, Lowry Air Force Base in Colorado, Loring Air Force Base in Maine, the Los Angeles Air Station in California, and a few other major facilities. To deal with these imminent closures, Carter proposed a new executive order whereby the federal government would provide adjustment assistance to these communities to ease the transition. Thanks to pressure from labor and peace groups, there is also a provision for prior planning—which was not in the original draft. It is still not an adequate program for conversion, but it is a small beginning. It says that we can go into these communities and do advance planning for the first time ever and try to demonstrate that this is a viable and workable process. We are seeing encouraging results, for example, at Fort Sheridan.

Local Projects

Fort Sheridan is a magnificent site north of Chicago. It has over a thousand civilian workers within the American Federation of Government Employees, which means a substantial amount of income flowing into the surrounding communities of Lake County. We went to Chicago and met with union representatives, the president of the Chamber of Commerce, school superintendents, staff people from Senator Stevenson's office, and other community leaders. We convinced them that they needed a contingency plan in case Fort Sheridan did close. As a result, the Lake County Board of Supervisors has applied for the federal government grants that are available for alternative-use planning, and a community advisory board is being set up with union leaders and area clergymen. This work done at Fort Sheridan is the very first attempt to do conversion planning at a military base. We hope that it will ease the difficult transition for Lake County, and we are trying to initiate the same process at Fort Dix and both Lowry and Loring Air Force Bases.

Another facility where conversion efforts are beginning is Bell Aerospace near Buffalo, New York, which has been involved in the Minuteman project. Thankfully, the Minuteman project is over, but now the workers face closure of that facility. People from our office visited their UAW local and told them about alternative-use planning. Now, they too are approaching the federal government and trying to get guidance from the UAW national office in Detroit. This conversion planning process is beginning at a number of other sites as well, and we hope to expand it many times over in the coming years.

In several communities around this country, there are very advanced conversion projects on the local level—for example, the Mid-Peninsula Conversion Project in California. It is in the Stanford area, which is one of the most heavily defense-dependent regions in the entire country. Approximately $2 billion worth of military contracts go into Santa Clara County every year, largely for military electronics.

The American Friends Service Committee of Santa Clara County supported an independent conversion project that is now being sponsored by the Central Labor Council in the area. They hope to establish an alternative-use planning committee for that whole county, with full cooperation from the local government—a very advanced step. In fact, they have just put out an important study on the conversion of the military industry to solar energy production, which shows that there is a substantial capability for converting military electronics operations to the manufacture of solar collectors, solar cells, and photovoltaic cells. That is the kind of vision that we need to inject into this whole discussion about the arms race.

We are really moving toward a new phase in our work. We are no longer the negative people—the "nay sayers." Now we are saying, "This is an enormous industrial asset that is being wasted on non-productive and inflation-causing military production. Let us convert it to those kinds of industries and activities which can lead toward a healthier and more productive civilian economy."

ARMS RACE—
COMMUNITY DECAY

Edward W. Rodman

We have to be concerned with a broader spectrum than just the infrastructure of the war economy and an analysis of how conversion can take place. We must also look at the human cost of continuing the present situation. Over this past year, I have had the rare privilege of working with a group called the Urban Bishop's Coalition of the Episcopal Church, one of whose projects was to sponsor a series of seven hearings in different cities around the country and in Colón, Panama. These hearings examined the state of our cities and the relationship of the church to urban concerns.

Recently, the Diocese of Massachusetts held a similar series of hearings in Lowell, Fall River, and Boston. Out of those experiences has come a rather concentrated dose of the human element involved in the continuation and perpetuation of the war economy, and what I like to call the "politics of avoidance." This is the politics that suggests, not only that we need a neutron bomb and a military-industrial complex, but also that we need more prisons and a death penalty. It is the kind of mentality that has led to the tax revolt which we now see in our society—a revolt threatening the kind of chaos and individualism which can only strengthen that "madness of immorality" described earlier by Dr. Brown.

The human cost of what is going on in society can be seen in many ways. As a matter of fact, there was a rather poignant scene on the

EDWARD W. RODMAN is Missioner to Minority Communities and a member, Bishop's staff, Episcopal Diocese of Massachusetts.

news showing President Carter and some of this country's black leaders, following a meeting to discuss the question of minority unemployment. It was clear that they had come to less than a meeting of the minds on what priority that subject should have in our society. In measured tones, we heard Vernon Jordan of the Urban League, and some of the others, indicate that not only is there unrest within our society because of the conditions that we are continually confronted with, but also there is a turning away from the established means of dealing with them. And that is the ultimate tragedy. You can talk about the physical blight in the cities and the human cost in terms of unemployment, but how do you deal with a situation where people have lost all hope?

The Throwaway Culture

One of the fascinating and very threatening issues that I see confronting us in the next few years—if we do not begin to make this a central issue in our culture—is the possibility that our society may come to the conclusion that it is tired of dealing with all of these social problems. In a book called *To Hear and to Heed,* which came out of the urban hearings, Dr. Joseph Pelham asks a very interesting and poignant question which bears on what ought to be one of the basic moral principles guiding our thoughts and actions in this whole area: "How does society deal with those who are no longer needed, or who are needed only as recipients of services? How do we deal with those whose existence constitutes, at best, an annoyance or, at worst, a threat?"[1]

One of the problems surrounding the whole argument of disarmament or conversion is that to be vindicated in your argument is to lose. What you must focus on are the alternatives which provide for a better society in which *all* people can live, and I think that is very important to understand. We live in a society whose war mentality translates itself into a domestic social policy which asks,

> Who *needs* those whose skills (or lack of skills) ill-suit them for a capital-intensive industrial system? Who *needs* those not prepared for participation in a work force that is now dominated by clerical, service, and office functions?
>
> Who *needs* welfare mothers? Who *needs* the young or the aged as anything but recipients of services? Who *needs* women who are bidding to be competitors for equal status in society? Who *needs* the threat raised by the sexual phobias written deep in the psyche of contemporary society and

[1] Joseph Pelham, "The Episcopal Church in the Urban Crisis: the Decade Ahead," *To Hear and to Heed* (Cincinnati: Forward Movement Publications, 1978), p. 43.

elicited by gays who insist that their sexual preferences and alternate life-styles be accepted, or who insist that gay rights have to do with the liberation of homosexual and heterosexual persons alike? Who in this consumption oriented society *needs* those whose poverty limits their ability to buy and to consume? Who *needs* the mentally or physically handicapped or the ill? Who *needs* those whose differences in language or culture put special demands and stresses on the equilibrium of white Anglo-Saxon culture?

Dr. Pelham points out that

this society has found an answer to those questions: The unneeded, under-valued, the threatening minorities are to be isolated, ghettoized, and contained. A "throw-away" culture has decided that the unneeded and threatening should be confined and labeled dispensable, except to the extent that they fulfill a necessary function as the under class. Economic, political and social decisions have been made to let the cities be the areas of confinement of this underclass.

But recent analyses and statistics have begun to show that even the cities are not going to be the place for this confinement and isolation, because the energy problem is bringing the white people back into those cities, displacing the poor and minorities. In Washington, D.C., alone, more than sixty thousand black persons have been lost from both the federal census and the city figures, and nobody knows what happened to them.

A Society for All

We are moving into a "crunch" period in our society and culture in which we are going to have to make some hard decisions. We are going to have to deal, not only with armaments and nuclear weapons, but with the entire fabric of our social policy that determines who survives and who does not. One of the fundamental problems of this whole movement is that it is a dialogue among essentially homogeneous people who see a threat in the long term, but who are not always concerned with the short-term pain of dealing with the problems as they exist in our society today.

A good friend of mine from seminary days is fond of saying that often, in movements and struggles of this kind, we have the blind leading the blind, without any visible results. One of the very real and basic issues that this effort must confront is how to incorporate the pain and suffering of minorities and others who are isolated and confined to our urban centers into our general concern for conversion. We must tap their energy, passion, and insights in order to make this a common struggle affecting the majority of the people in this society, not only those whose intellectual or moral principles happen to be consistent with yours.

I am sure all of you are familiar with *The Poseidon Adventure,* that movie where the luxury liner was sailing along until a tidal wave turned it over. I saw that movie with my daughter, who was four or five years old at the time, and afterward I asked her how she liked it. She said, "Daddy, it was a great movie until the ship turned over." Out of the mouths of babes comes wisdom. You see, it is a great movie for the military-industrial complex and for the decision makers in this society, but until we turn that ship over and begin the real struggle of defining life in human terms, we have missed the point.

STANDING UP TO THE PENTAGON

George A. Athanson

I have felt for a very long time that the basic problem in this country is that we do not know what the real problems are. We make erroneous assumptions, reach wrong conclusions, and squander our money all over the world supporting reactionary regimes. And the basic problem since the Second World War has been that we have not connected domestic policy with foreign policy. No president since the time of that war—Republican or Democrat, "Republicrat" or "Demonican"—has fully understood that relationship.

For example, President Johnson had the Great Society in which there were tremendous surges forward toward solving the urban crisis in our country, but he got bogged down in Vietnam because he did not comprehend the linkages between domestic and foreign policy. The way that we perceive the world determines our defense budget, and what determines our defense budget determines our domestic priorities. I am saying that we are wrong on all counts. Our perception of the world is wrong, and we have wrong domestic priorities because we are emphasizing our defense budget—constant rises, even during peace.

William Miller, chairman of the Federal Reserve Board, in a speech given in Hartford, Connecticut, said that the reason for our current inflation is Vietnam. Because President Johnson refused to

GEORGE A. ATHANSON is mayor of Hartford, Connecticut, and a former professor of history, political science, and international relations, University of Hartford.

call for a tax increase to take care of the approximately $33 billion a year being spent in Vietnam at that time, the cities of America—where most of the poor reside—are really paying for the Vietnam War today. We made wrong assumptions, reached erroneous conclusions, and it is said that over $500 billion will be the total spent on Vietnam, including veterans' benefits, pensions, and so forth.

One-Dimensional Policy

Our involvement in Indo-China started with President Truman and increased with every succeeding president. Our posture with respect to the world has been determined since 1947 by the "Truman Doctrine"—military containment. It is a "Republicratic-Demonican" foreign policy. But the tragedy in our country is that we are not really a democracy when it comes to foreign policy, because there are no alternatives being discussed by any political party. That is the real problem.

When the state legislature of Connecticut took half of the polluted Connecticut River away from Hartford and gave it to the neighboring town of East Hartford, I submitted a press release to the papers protesting the move. It is polluted, but it had been our river for three hundred years! So I said, "I'll show you," and I got the Trinity College crew team with their boat, and the Hartford Police Department, whose boat had a big leak in it. I had a woman prepare a flag—the only flag of the city of Hartford—and I burst forth like George Washington crossing the Delaware. I was in the bow of the Trinity College boat and I put the public media (the television people) in the boat with the leak in it—which almost sank in the middle of the crossing.

When we got to the other side, the press asked me, "Why did you do it?" I said, "Well, you're here. This is an urban crisis, but instead of giving publicity to the fact that water—even polluted water—was taken away from a central city, you relegated that crisis to the obituary page of the newspaper. People have got to know the nature and depth of the crisis in which we find ourselves." That is a big part of the problem.

But the problem really goes deeper, because I do not foresee either the Republican or the Democratic Party doing that which is essential in terms of reordering our priorities, either domestically, or in terms of our foreign policy. I see the need for a grass-roots movement like the March on Washington initiated by Dr. Martin Luther King, Jr., with labor people, minorities, and other progressive citizens working together.

I am not interested in a demonstration project on conversion in "Podunk, U.S.A." I am interested in national programs to resolve national problems. I am not interested in President Carter saying, "We will give you twenty-five demonstration cities to undertake the problem of unemployed youth." I am interested in employment for all of America's youth, especially in the inner city. But Carter cannot do that, because he has promised to raise the defense budget 3 percent above the inflation rate. That is his solution for conquering inflation, but you know that the more you increase the defense budget, the more inflation you get! You are really killing your own anti-inflation program by increasing defense expenditures.

Furthermore, the Public Interest Research Group in Michigan made a study of jobs and defense, and it turns out that the more defense work you have, the fewer jobs you have. It is not the other way around. This is even true in Connecticut—in highly industrialized areas where defense expenditures are paramount. That is the problem.

Global Perceptions

I am concerned that the way in which we perceive the world helps to determine our defense budget, and our perceptions have been erroneous since the Second World War. You cannot have a Truman Doctrine to stop Communism—to "contain" it—because in essence you are really helping to spread it. We lost in Vietnam because we made erroneous assumptions and wrong conclusions and threw billions and billions of dollars into the pot to fight something that we could not win. And who suffered in the process? The poor in our cities and the poor in the Third World have suffered as a result of our misguided efforts.

What is it about the American character that determines how we perceive the world? Gabriel Almond, in his book, *The American People and Foreign Policy,* looks into the psycho-cultural characteristics of the American people. Almond talks about us being aggressive, individualistic, atomistic, and materialistic, and says we are usually aggressive for materialistic purposes. We perceive the world the way we do because of the American value structure, which leads us to support reactionary regimes like the Shah of Iran. We forget that there are people with religious feelings and intellectual yearnings—people who care about where their customs and traditions are going. And our Central Intelligence Agency—which should be renamed "the Central Stupid Agency"—fails to comprehend our current position realistically.

This whole situation reflects our inability to comprehend and understand the forces of history, and because we learn nothing from the historical past, we are doomed to repeat mistakes again and again; as we have. Meanwhile, where is the discussion? There is none. We talk about human rights, but when it comes to our allies—Korea, Marcos in the Philippines, South Africa, Iran, Turkey, refugees on the island of Cyprus—we say relatively nothing because they are our friends. Our national security is paramount, so the hell with human rights! A moral principle has to be applied everywhere without fear or favor if it is going to be endowed with that human spirit that was the spirit of the Lord. That is the only way it can be done.

The Need for Change

What is the way out? How can we possibly get out of this "valley of the shadow of death" where we find ourselves? How can we try to reach the mountaintop? Where is the salvation?

First of all, education is extremely important, which is why convocations of this kind must be held. Secondly, we must reestablish the coalition of concerned people, labor, minorities, and citizens working together for the common good. We have got to point out that our cities are suffering because of the inability to comprehend the relationships and the linkages that exist between domestic and foreign policy. We have to point out how our youth are suffering as a result. It is not enough to say "Humphrey-Hawkins" and not allocate any money. This is only symbolic. It is not enough to go to the president and ask, "What are you going to do for the poor today, Mr. President?" And the president says, "Ah, don't worry. I am going to raise the defense budget by 3 percent over the inflation rate." Two weeks later, you try it again—repeating the same syndrome over and over.

The die has been cast. This administration has made its fundamental choice, and that choice is guns over butter, which means more inflation and more problems for the cities of America. It means that when you plan your city budget, inflation is going to hit, followed by recession and joblessness. And you know where people are going to go—not to the president (he has a big iron fence and the Secret Service all around). They are going to go to the mayors of America. I have an open-door policy. I am out there day and night, seven days a week, eighteen hours a day, with the people! That is my moral responsibility, not to be cut off by iron fences, but to be with the people listening to what they have to say.

Our basic problem is that we have not linked local, state, and federal governments with international relationships in a creative way. We say, "Get more money from the state," but that is not the answer. We may save Connecticut, but the problems of Massachusetts will soon encroach upon Connecticut, New York, New Jersey, and Pennsylvania. We cannot save one part of the country at the expense of another. Salvation must be total; that means internationally, nationally, at the state level, and locally. It cannot be done

William Sloane Coffin, Jr., offers a present of Vermont maple syrup as a gift to the children at the Soviet Embassy, presenting it to Soviet First Secretary Yuri Kapralov.

piecemeal. Unless we are all saved, not one of us can be saved. That is the point, and what we need is a concerted effort.

I see no alternative to the Republican and Democratic parties unless the Democratic Party is captured, but there are too many southern representatives now, and when you have the "Plains Syndrome," you are very limited. Some of the same things that have made us a great nation may very well cause our decline and fall—democracy, individualism, private property. We say that freedom of speech and freedom of the press are rights we believe in and are ready to die for. But you cannot preach the Bill of Rights to the poor in southeastern or northeastern Brazil who are making fifty dollars a year, or to the poor in Africa or Southeast Asia. They will not know what you are talking about. They might well ask, "Can you eat the Bill of Rights? Our stomachs are bloated; we need sustenance. Freedom of speech, what is it? I don't understand what you are talking about."

How then do we bring about basic change? There is only one way—what we did in 1776. Our basic problem is that we have turned our backs on our historical heritage and as a result, we have to squander billions and billions of dollars because we have put our faith in arms. They are supposed to give us security, but the more money we spend on those arms, the less secure we become. We start turning against each other and we think of cults to save us—some great leader in whom we can put our faith—because there is no other way to salvation.

I fear the possibility of fascism in this country. I am concerned. I discussed some of these issues at the National League of Cities, and the reply was, "Oh, that's foreign policy; that's the Executive Branch." At the U.S. Conference of Mayors, I passed a resolution several years ago to discuss domestic and foreign policy, but it has never been put into effect. Even on the local level, we do not understand. We have got to march like we did in Washington. We have got to work as a permanent coalition to see what we can do with the political party structure, and if that does not work, we may have to think about an alternative party system that can bring about the basic changes which are essential.

When history is written a thousand years from now and the historians ask, "When did the change really begin to take place?"—somebody will answer, "Riverside Church, December, 1978!" Is it a wild dream? No! God marches on, and he needs his disciples to be with him so all of us can change the world for his kingdom and for humanity.

PEACE
IN SEARCH OF
MAKERS.

A public liturgy at The Riverside Church, 490 Riverside Drive at 122nd. Street. Monday, Dec. 4 at 8.30 pm. **W**ith Pete Seeger, Dr. Benjamin Spock, Congressman Ronald V. Dellums and Dr. William Sloane Coffin, Jr.

REVERSE
THE ARMS
RACE.

The Riverside Church Disarmament Program
New York City (212) 749-7000, Ext. 148

A public liturgy held in the nave of Riverside Church dramatized the need to reverse the arms race. The evening of politics, theater, music, and theology also included Peter Seeger, the Reverend Fred Kirkpatrick, Pearl Williams Jones, and Ralph Lee's Giant Puppets.

Peace in Search of Makers

Calls to Peace:	Dr. Eugene Laubach	—Riverside Church
	Placida Robinson	—Riverside Church
	Dr. James Forbes	—Union Theological Seminary
	Edith Lerrigo	—Riverside Church
	Rabbi Balfour Brickner	—Union of American Hebrew Congregations
	Sister Ardeth Platte	—Saginaw, Michigan, City Council
	Dr. Benjamin Spock	—Pediatrician and peace activist
Confession:	Rev. Evelyn Newman	
Litany		
Sermon:	"The Things That Make for Peace. . . ." Rev. William Sloane Coffin, Jr.	
Testimony:	"There is Another Way." . . . Congressman Ronald V. Dellums	

LITURGY: "PEACE IN SEARCH OF MAKERS"

CALLS FOR PEACE

Dr. Eugene Laubach

It is the moral responsibility of the church to call for peace. A good many of you here probably remember Dwight Eisenhower saying, "The hunger for peace is too great for any government to mock men's hopes with mere words and promises and gestures." He recognized how badly the people of our world desired peace. But that was twenty-five years ago, and we are no nearer to a peaceful world today. In fact, every weapon that comes off the assembly line—supposedly those that are geared to protect us and make us feel more secure—brings the threat of nuclear disaster that much closer.

It is time to stop this insane competition to come up with the *most*, the *biggest*, the *deadliest*, and the most accurate weapons in the world. But if our national leaders are unwilling to take that significant first step toward winding down the arms race, then those of us who are charged with moral leadership must take the initiative. We must voice the doubts and concerns that others find it impossible to utter. The Bible says, "Blessed are the peacemakers, for they shall be called the children of God." Let us start looking for those children of God right now, by issuing our call for peace.

Placida Robinson

I am sixteen years old. There are a lot of things in this world that I am just waiting to experience. And to me, one heavy word is "life."

Isn't it beautiful just to wake up and feel the sunshine, or go to bed and see the stars? These things to me are beautiful, just as God created a beautiful earth. There is no reason to destroy it now. Why should we go on, ninety miles an hour, destroying ourselves, when it is God who created us? I want to go out and experience many of the same things that your children want to do. I want to raise my own kids and show them my experiences. I want an education. I would like to live comfortably. I would like to live in a safe world at peace. And I would like to live in love, because love is what we need to bind us together. The only things I want to feel from the sky are the sunshine and the rain, not bombs or any other concoction created just to go out and have more power. Because the love of power is destroying the power of love.

Dr. James Forbes

I speak of peace from the perspective of people who, during this time of the year that we call Advent, speak a lot about peace on earth in the name of One whom they call the Prince of Peace. So, in a community gathering calling for peace, surely we should have a clear word to offer. But there are many perspectives, for different voices appealing to different Scriptures point us this way and then the other.

Some remind us, "Remember when He said, 'Things are getting so bad that those of you who don't have a sword had better go out and get one'?"

Another voice says, "No, but remember that on one occasion He only heard the disciples say, 'We have two swords.' And He said, 'That's enough.'"

Yet another said, "Well, when the showdown came, even the one who took the sword and cut off the high priest's servant's ear heard him say, 'Put the sword away.' And then after He experienced the sword, came forth again saying, 'My peace I give unto you not as the world gives.'"

So out of all these voices, what have we to say during the season of peace? I think I put it together this way: First, the reason one is told to "go and get a sword if you don't have one" is that there comes a time when being oblivious to the serious nature of the human experiment is unforgivable, and in order to alert the world to the seriousness of the crisis, it was necessary for the Prince of Peace to say, "Look, it is serious enough that you had better get ready to encounter conflict on every hand."

And then, when this call is made, "two swords, is this enough?" He says, "Yes, I think that is enough." I think that is simply his acknowledgment that most of us have certain security needs, and we would probably retreat before the battle even got started unless there were some sign of security.

But why put the swords away when the battle has come? Because my battle draws from a source of power that the world does not yet know. Therefore, I hear him saying, "I tested it—the plan of peace based on love, power, and justice may cause you to come to a moment when vulnerability may be the direction in which you go." But having tested the plan, he reported that any one who started the plan is capable of following it through.

And therefore the call to peace tonight comes this way. Those of you who are ready, you are asked to take a stand, where you can, in relation to that plan, but remain open in regard to the position you take. For if the Spirit that leads you into truth finds you, what may happen if the Spirit "gets on your case" is that your old standing place may become a disgrace because you're running in the wrong race. So we are here to know and to grow; and then don't sit there on the mark; get ready, get set, and go. . . . for peace!

Edith Lerrigo

I am a senior citizen. I am retired and trying to live on a fixed income. Those of you who are working know, when you go into a store—a department store or supermarket—what it means when prices go up. So you can imagine what it means for those of us on fixed incomes—and there are thousands and thousands in this city—when prices go up.

As citizens and taxpayers, we have made a contract with our government. We have agreed to pay taxes in exchange for services given to us. We have worked hard. We have paid our taxes, and I think we must expect of our government that they supply the services we need in return for what we give. But instead, friends, instead, we see our money going into weapons systems— more every year—and less going into meeting the social needs of the people of this country and the world.

In fact, I recently read an article telling about how our president asked that next year's defense budget be more than $120 billion, but he also asked that social programs be cut by $15 billion. And you know what that means: Health care, Medicaid, Medicare, and Social Security are the programs that will be affected. If we do not reverse our priorities and spend more on helping people with their needs instead of worrying about defending them, we're not going to have very much left to defend.

Those of us who are old remember that they called the First World War the "war to end all wars." But I'm afraid that the next war, if we have one, will be the war to end all.

Rabbi Balfour Brickner

"Lo yisa goy el goy herev." In the words of the prophet Isaiah, "Nation shall not lift up sword against nation, neither shall they learn war anymore."

"Shalom, Shalom, v'ein Shalom." Words also from the prophet Jeremiah: "'Peace, peace,' when there is no peace."

We wish for peace; we yearn for peace; we pray for peace. "Grant us peace, thy most precious gift, O Thou eternal source of peace. Enable us to be its messenger unto the peoples of the earth." These are words from the liturgy of the Jewish Prayer Book.

But we work at war, or we are preparing for it, and we justify those deeds in the name of defense. How shall we be messengers of peace unto the peoples of the earth, on the tip of a missile or the nose of a neutron-laden shell? We are caught in a terrible polarity. Frustration is our constant companion. The peaceful world we seek for ourselves and our children cannot be built without sacrifice. It can be established now only at the cost of great and painful renunciations— the renunciation by every people on earth of the idolatrous patriotism which puts nation above humanity and even the place of God. It means renunciation of the fears, suspicions, and prejudices that set race against race, people against people, and that enkindle flames of fierce hatred among one another; the renunciation of avarice, the renunciation of our impulses in times of personal and collective frustration to strike out in fury, the renunciation of arrogance and blindness—that which closes our eyes to the nobility and goodness and truth that reside within each of us.

Is the price of peace too great? Are we yet sufficiently mature? There is an iron, unbreakable law, that when a world civilization comes to an end, its end is brought about by its own folly, not by its enemies. If the decline of our world is at hand, it is not because of Communism, but because free men are destroying their own best hopes. We are destroying that hope which is our children, that hope which is their faith in a better world. Will we be able to find a better way?

Could one hold a convocation like this without words from the sainted and beloved Abraham Heschel, whose presence pervades this hallowed sanctuary as it hallows our presence: "It seems as though we have arrived at a period of a divine eclipse in human history. We sail the seas, we count the stars, we split the atom. We never ask, 'Is there nothing but a dead universe and our reckless curiosity?'"

Horrified by the discovery of man's power to bring about the annihilation of organic life on this planet, we are today beginning to comprehend that the sense of the sacred is as vital to us as is the light of the sun; that the enjoyment of beauty, possessions, and safety in civilized society depends on men's and women's sense of the sacredness of life. The basic foundation upon which our cities stand is a handful of spiritual ideas. All of our life hangs by a thread—the faithfulness of man to the concern of God.

God is the subject of all subjects. Life is his and ours. I will conclude with this story: A righteous man was going from Sodom to Gomorrah to rebuke the people for their evil deeds. A passerby mocked him, "You know that no one will pay you any heed. You can never make them as you are." "I know," he answered, "but at least by speaking out, I will not become as they are."

Sister Ardeth Platte

I wish to make a brief request of this religious convocation. When we begin to develop our strategy to reverse the arms race, let it start with our rejection of any support for SALT II.

For one thing, it is not a step in the direction of reversing the arms race. It is an invitation to the Soviets to increase the number of their delivery vehicles. Secondly, it does not in any way limit the qualitative arms race. It allows for continuing technological research. This is leading more and more toward making nuclear war thinkable. Thirdly, our support of SALT II is legitimizing it, giving our blessing to the present posture of mutual assured destruction.

On January 1, 1976, Pope Paul VI called the bombing of Hiroshima, "a butchery of untold magnitude." If we agree with that moral judgment, how in the name of God can we give any support to an agreement that provides for the United States to maintain an arsenal with the destructive power of 615,000 Hiroshima bombs? Let us agree to say "no" to SALT II and demand instead that we truly get on with the task of reversing the arms race. Our challenge is one like Jesus', to organize on the streets, to work for justice, to preserve life for young and old in our cities and on our farmlands. It is necessary to organize ourselves, and to move firmly, consistently, and urgently toward peace. Amen.

Dr. Benjamin Spock

One of the frightening things I learned from participating in the opposition to the Vietnam War was that, though the federal government may be made up of individuals, the majority of whom are reasonably intelligent and honest, the conglomeration is unbelievably timid and cowardly, bowing to lobbyists, fearful of losing face, and incapable of facing the evidence.

Presidents, secretaries of defense, generals, and most of the Senate and House could not get it through their heads that small, undeveloped Vietnam would refuse to be conquered by the world's most powerful nation. After World War II, the French tried to reimpose colonial control and were ignominiously defeated. Eisenhower and Dulles thought they could do better. They installed and supported a puppet who failed miserably. Kennedy sent twenty thousand military advisors who made no progress. When Johnson's turn came, he declared, "I refuse to be the first president to lose a war," and sent a half-million fighting troops, 55,000 of whom died. Though he and his advisors—McNamara, the Bundys, the Rostows—were considered smart fellows, they too failed, and Johnson had to give up the presidency.

Nixon continued the carnage for five more years, because he said the world would consider us "a helpless giant" if we quit. Eventually, the Vietnamese pushed our army and our puppets out. Meanwhile, more and more millions of Americans had come to see that the war was unwinnable, but our Pentagon and our successive administrations were the very last to catch on. They were still making inane predictions of victory right up until the end.

My plea to you civilians who are willing to think for yourselves is to free yourselves from that compulsion left over from childhood to assume that the government is wise because it is so big and powerful, and to realize that it is just a monstrous colony—as they say of a coral reef—with no overall sense of direction. Its various parts respond automatically to the pressures of special interests. Industry loves defense contracts; so does labor, and so does the local press in the cities where the contracts are awarded. Congressmen are given some of the credit for contract awards, which helps them at election time.

As long as all groups appear to be enthusiastic about great defense budgets, there will be no disarmament and there will be no limitation. A reversal of the trend will come only if enough citizens become alarmed at the certainty of national bankruptcy or nuclear annihilation and build a truly powerful lobby for disarmament. The only question is, "Which will come first?"

CONFESSION

The Reverend Evelyn Newman

Let us pray. O Thou Almighty God, even as we come now before Thee, we stand under the shadow of the bomb. Words come slowly. It is too terrible to contemplate. Our children play; our women give birth under the shadow of the bomb. We brush it quickly from our minds like a nightmare; we don't want to dwell on it. We pretend it isn't there, and romp on this volcano of our own making.

O God, have mercy on us. As a sophisticated people, saintliness makes us uneasy. We are more at home with strategy. As an intelligent people, we have freed ourselves from naive religious myths, but we are caught in the dangerous myth that nuclear weapons are not meant to be used. As a moral people, we are ashamed to cry, "An eye for an eye." But with reason and judgment, we endorse a bomb for a bomb in an ever-escalating arms race.

O God, how quickly we can make hell out of heaven. Must we grope for words to express our anguish? Dost Thou not see the faces of pain turn toward Thee? Bloated budgets, bloated bellies, burned-out buildings, burned-out souls. We cry for love; we cry for sanity; we cry for peace. And, O God, how we cry for the lack of peace!

Lord, do we not want peace enough to let our prayer be answered? Is it that we so easily conjure up images of enemies and project blame on Thee so we will not have to face the things that make for war within ourselves? Is it that we want peace only as it serves our own purposes as individuals? As governments? As transnational corporations?

O God, forgive us. Forgive us for relinquishing moral leadership, for believing in the inevitability and the legitimacy of war, for placing our faith in a hopeless security system, for passively giving over to the Pentagon power to cause our own destruction. Forgive us, O God, and demand accountability from us so that it shall no longer be the blind leading the blind over the abyss of disaster. Give us the wisdom to follow our leaders only insofar as they are obedient to Thee. Let the words, "Thy will be done" never again signal submission to any state or any lesser authority, but let them forever be reserved for Thee and Thee alone.

We who have put this dark cloud in Thy heavens, in deepest sorrow, make our confessions before Thee and before each other. Gracious God, living, loving Spirit, now in the silence of our own souls, call each one of us by name, and call us out as a people of peace. Hear the prayer, O God, of the people who stand under the shadow of the bomb, and make us instruments of Thy peace. Amen.

LITANY

Featured Players:
  Mr. Military-Industrial Complex
  Mr. & Mrs. America
  Citizens

MR. MILITARY-INDUSTRIAL COMPLEX: I would like to improve my—excuse me—*our* Intercontinental Ballistic Missiles. We are developing a nuclear warfare strategy and we have only 550 of the missiles now, hidden in silos around the country. I'd like to double their explosive power and their accuracy. This would give us the ability to knock out the enemy's hardened missile silos and other military targets—just in case we ever need to strike first. I'll need about $335 million for starters. What do you say?

MR. & MRS. AMERICA: Well, if you spend that much on missiles, it means cutting back on social programs. In fact, next year's budget shows a cut of $15 billion in social services, but no cuts from defense spending. We happen to feel that this money would be better spent on things such as education. When you consider the number of schools around this country with inadequate facilities and shrinking budgets, the quality of education can't help but be affected. When you consider that the U.S. ranks number one in the world in military might, but fifteenth in literacy. We think . . .

MR. MILITARY-INDUSTRIAL COMPLEX: You'd better think again!

MR. & MRS. AMERICA *(silence):*

MR. MILITARY-INDUSTRIAL COMPLEX *(sarcastically):* Thanks . . . I would also like the neutron bomb. It only costs $1.5 billion. It's small and neat and very effective. The great thing about it, of course, is that it kills *people,* but leaves property virtually untouched. You see, it attacks the central nervous system causing nausea, diarrhea, and convulsions. If the dose is strong enough, some people die immediately, while others linger for two or three months before becoming delirious, falling into a coma and . . . expiring.

MR. & MRS. AMERICA: But the housing situation in this country is atrocious. Five years ago, seventeen million Americans were living in deprived housing, including 28 percent of the houses right here in the New York area, and things certainly haven't improved since then.

Mr. Pentagoon represented the Military Industrial Complex, pleading for funds to build bigger weapons. Ralph Lee's Giant Puppets illustrated the refusal of Americans to spend their taxes for war.

Why, a lot of the houses people are forced to live in don't even deserve to stay standing.

MR. MILITARY-INDUSTRIAL COMPLEX: Just be quiet and give me the money so I can build these weapons.

CITIZENS: NOT WITH *OUR* TAXES YOU DON'T!

MR. MILITARY-INDUSTRIAL COMPLEX *(flustered):* I want the cruise missile. It's great. It can be launched from land, sea, or air. It's like a small, pilotless plane, fifteen or twenty feet long, that can fly at tree-top level, too low to be detected by enemy radar. As one official from General Dynamics put it, "It's like shoving a grenade down the other guy's throat." What's more, it's cheap. Only $1 million apiece. I'd like five thousand of them. That's only $5 billion. It'll be very good for Boeing and General Dynamics, too.

MR. & MRS. AMERICA: We don't care if it's going to be good for Boeing and General Dynamics. We know it won't do *us* any good, and in the long run, it won't even do their workers any good. It will simply make the companies more dependent on the Pentagon—*on you*—and when budget cuts come, it won't be management that will bear the brunt; it will be individual workers and their families and communities. If there were rational planning for converting military industries to peacetime production, that wouldn't happen. Believe us, there are lots of needs in this society that aren't being met by corporations.

MR. MILITARY-INDUSTRIAL COMPLEX: Shut up. I want the cruise missile. If you give me the money, I can protect your lives.

CITIZENS: NOT *OUR* LIVES YOU DON'T!

MR. MILITARY-INDUSTRIAL COMPLEX: *(enraged):* I need the Trident submarine. It will cost more than $30 billion. It will be the largest submarine human beings have ever built. It's as long as two football fields and five stories high. It will carry many hundreds of nuclear warheads, and it will allow me to take the offensive in a nuclear war. With this monster—uh, weapon—I can patrol the whole world.

MR. & MRS. AMERICA: Why not hollow one out and turn it into a 200-bed hospital? It's big enough, and the need is surely there. Why, right here in New York City, Lincoln Hospital desperately needs $3 million added to its yearly budget, just to be able to function adequately. How about giving them $3 million instead of building your submarines?

MR. MILITARY-INDUSTRIAL COMPLEX: Give me the Trident! We can ring the world with nuclear weapons.

CITIZENS: NOT *OUR* WORLD YOU DON'T!

MR. MILITARY-INDUSTRIAL COMPLEX *(enraged):* I need the MX—It's really an incredible subway for missiles . . .

MR. & MRS. AMERICA: Subways are for people . . .

MR. MILITARY-INDUSTRIAL COMPLEX *(flailing):* I need the MX. I must have $225 from every child, woman, and man in this audience. I command you to give it to me now!

CITIZENS:NO!
> NOT WITH *OUR* TAXES
> NOT WITH *OUR* LIVES
> NOT WITH *OUR* WORLD

SERMON

"The Things That Make for Peace"

William Sloane Coffin, Jr.

Let me begin by reading one of the most poignant sections of Scripture. In the Palm Sunday scene, when Christ and the disciples draw near to the center of the Mount of Olives, the whole multitude begins to rejoice and praise God with a loud voice for all the mighty works they have seen. They say: "Blessed is the King who comes in the name of the Lord! Peace in heaven and glory in the highest." At this point some of the Pharisees in the multitude say to him, "Teacher, rebuke your disciples." But Christ answers, "I tell you, if these were silent, the very stones would cry out." And when he draws near and sees the city, he weeps over it saying, "Would that even today you knew the things that make for peace." (See Luke 19:38-42.)

The Bonds of Sin

Let us consider some of those things that make for peace. We have heard an idea implied again and again at this convocation, namely, that you do not divide the world up into good guys and bad guys— "children of light and children of darkness." It is the old Manichean heresy, and there are two terrible things at the heart of it. First, you fight evil as if it were something that rose totally outside of yourself, and secondly, you deny your enemy his humanity. You have to love

WILLIAM SLOANE COFFIN, JR., is Senior Minister, the Riverside Church.

your enemy, in part because you made him that way. We must always see our complicity in the very evils that we abhor.

For example, it is perfectly true that the Soviets are armed to the teeth, but we were the first to develop the atom bomb, the usable hydrogen bomb, the ICBM, the Cruise Missile, before that the Poseidon, and now, the Trident. So while it is true that *they* are armed to the teeth, *we* certainly had a part in it. Then, too, the Soviets are meddling all over the world. Never mind what they are doing in Africa; what they did in Czechoslovakia was terrible, and in Hungary in 1956, and in East Germany back in 1953.

But let us consider our own record. Since 1945, we have intervened militarily, or in a major CIA operation, in the internal affairs of a small country on an average of once every eighteen months. Count them up: 1948, Greece; 1953, Iran; 1954, Guatemala; 1958, Indonesia; 1958, Lebanon; 1960, Laos; 1961, Cuba; 1964, the Congo; 1964, British Guiana; 1965, Dominican Republic; and after that, Vietnam and Chile.

The message is clear. If nations are not bound one to another in love, at least they are bound together in sin. And it is no mean bond, for it precludes the possibility of separation through judgment. We are too criminal to judge. We are all involved in it. And what a beautiful thing it is to recognize that.

I can picture, in my evening fantasies, Andrei Gromyko and Cyrus Vance getting together, and I hear Vance say, "Oh, Andrei, if you only knew how we have sinned in the United States." Then Gromyko answers, "Oh, Cyrus, you haven't done anything compared to what we have done." What a marvelous beginning that would be to some truly fruitful negotiations!

Confession is good for the soul, and it is good for the souls of nations. If we are not bound together in love, at least let us recognize that we are bound, one to another, in sin. But that is not enough. In fact, it's too easy—although not too easy to recognize sometimes.

Human Unity

Our harder task is to try to be bound together in love. Let us resolve, as we go forth from this conference, to hate the evil, but not as much as we love the good. We hate the evil *only* because we so love the good. I also hope that we can go forth with a thorough rejection of any type of tribalistic chauvinism, for it is clear that the survival unit in our time is not an individual nation or an individual anything. The survival unit in our time is the entire human race plus its environment, which is not a new discovery. It is the discovery of something old—as old as all the major religions of the world. It is something that we have always proclaimed: that we all belong one to another. That is the way God made us, and Christ died to keep us that way. Our sin is only that we continue to put asunder what God himself has joined together.

Am I my brother's keeper? No—I am my brother's brother. Human unity is not even something that we are called on to create. It is only something we are called on to recognize. So let us remember, not only are we bound one to another in sin, we also have a basic unity which needs to be confirmed, particularly at times when nations want to tear it apart.

But it is not enough to talk about a global future as Henry Kissinger used to do, or as corporations do today. In fact, they say national boundaries are no more interesting to them than the equator. The issue of these multinational corporations is a complicated one, and I do not think we can solve it by reducing it to a simple moral formula. That being said, however, I think we must recognize that the Henry Kissingers of the world and the corporation presidents—all the rich and powerful—tend to see themselves as village elders in the "Global Village." They tend also to be more concerned with disorder than with injustice, which inevitably produces more of both.

Love and Justice

We have to proclaim not merely a global future, but a *just* and global future. Justice is to our own time the same moral imperative as freedom of speech was to Europe a hundred years ago. So let us decide that we will not only be bound in sin. We will also recognize our unity and strive to be bound *by* love and *in* justice.

Furthermore, the anti-Communists need to be exposed. If they were serious about fighting Communism, they would fight poverty, illiteracy, and sickness, because Communism thrives as a parasite—a disease in the body politic all around the world. But instead, the anti-Communists go for military solutions which have been tried again and again and have failed again and again. Why don't they learn from Lenin, who was successful, not because he was a Marxist, but because he said, "Peace, Land, and Bread." That was the great slogan that went right to the heart of the needs of the Russian people. Why can't we resurrect that type of thing? We must be able to see that anti-Communism is not the opposite of Communism. It is the opposite of social change. Fear of Communism is merely a camouflage for conservatives.

Let me reaffirm once again that we must strive to be bound, not only in sin, but in love and justice. And we must not grow weary. In the words of Isaiah, "Let us run and not grow weary." True, the road ahead is long and rough. True, we will have to duplicate conferences like this time and time again in city after city. We will have to approach city councils and congressmen, and there will be demonstrations of various kinds. And ultimately we may fail, but right now, we have scarcely tried. We may fail, but we must never act as if failure were morally justified.

Then again, who knows? By the grace of God, we may succeed in making our world a true homeland for humanity. Maybe we shall succeed in addressing the better self that is present in all of us. Maybe the world will remember that its poor are precious in the sight of God. Maybe the world will even remember its children. *"Los niños son la esperanza del futuro del mundo,"* said the great José Martí. (Children are the hope of the future of the world.) They deserve to inherit the world. We must leave it to them.

So let us run and not grow weary; walk and not faint. Not until that day when, by God's grace, faith and hope will be outdistanced by sight and possession, and love will be all in all, in this wonderful, terrible, beautiful world. Amen.

TESTIMONY

"There Is Another Way"

Ronald V. Dellums

Brothers and sisters, I am pleased, honored, and proud to be here this evening, because truth is being spoken, peace is being advocated, love is being expressed, and education is taking place—an incredible evening.

It is incredible for me because it is extraordinarily lonely confronting expediency in the United States Congress, so it is always good to know that there are tens of thousands of people who believe the same as we believe. It is also an incredible source of strength, because it is not frightened people who will lead this nation and change the destiny of the world, but only people who understand the

RONALD V. DELLUMS is a member, U.S. House of Representatives (D—Calif.); Secretary, Black Caucus; Member, Armed Services Committee.

love, and the humanism, and the strength that come with advocating truth and advocating peace.

This is a significant evening because when you look around this room, whether you know it or not, there are potentially ten tons of TNT lying there waiting to blow each and every one of you off the face of the earth. Now what do I mean by that? I mean that when you combine the explosive power of the United States and the Soviet Union, you get between ten and twelve tons of TNT for every man, woman, and child that walks the face of the earth; so each of you in this room has your own private ten tons of TNT to blow you to smithereens. That terrible potential is one reason why tonight is significant.

Tonight is also significant because by the year 1980, our military budget could exceed $140 billion, and by 1985, it could be as high as $200 billion. Clearly, we are at a point in time when there are incredible issues that need to be dealt with and discussed.

This is a significant evening because the neutron bomb blurs the distinction between conventional weapons and strategic weapons. It makes nuclear war thinkable, acceptable, possible, and—in my estimation—ultimately inevitable.

This is a significant evening because the cruise missile is an arms controller's nightmare.

This is a significant evening because we, as human beings, have more responsibility than any other living organism on the face of this earth. We are the only living organism that has the potential to destroy all life on earth, and that brings an awesome, disquieting, and disturbing responsibility to each of us.

This is a significant evening because many generations have said, "This is the important generation." But *this is* the important generation, because we have now achieved the technology to destroy everything on the face of this earth. You and I sitting in this room have in our hands the destiny of America and the destiny of the world.

This is a significant evening because today belongs to *us,* but as the Reverend Coffin pointed out eloquently, "Tomorrow belongs to the children." And if you believe as I believe, that a society which is not capable of addressing the concerns of its children is a society destined to die, then tonight is significant.

If you agree with me that a society which is not humanistic is a society destined to die, then tonight is a significant evening.

If you agree with me that a society which is not capable of embracing humanistic values is a society not worth saving, then tonight is a significant evening.

The Quickening Pace of the Arms Race

Tonight is a significant evening because it points out that there are enormous domestic issues going begging because we continue to build a monument to military madness, death, and destruction.

Tonight is a significant evening because you are beginning to learn—those of you who did not know before—that the problems of the world today are rapidly becoming political problems which we cannot solve by military solutions. Military power, bombs, and missiles cannot bring down the price of oil. Big bombs and military power cannot bring peace to the Middle East. Big bombs and military power cannot bring black majority rule to southern Africa. These are political issues which do not lend themselves to military solutions.

And finally, tonight is a significant evening because it gives us an opportunity to pause for a moment and understand that there is a right-wing analysis of America's problems which is permeating the American political scene, and which is going unchallenged in this country. It is an analysis that is anti-black, anti-brown, anti-red, anti-yellow, anti-women, anti-young, anti-old, anti-consumer, pro-corporations, and pro-militarism—a right-wing analysis that American media is projecting as representative of the majority of the American people. And I resent it.

The majority of the American people have not moved further to the Right, but if we do not challenge the insanity of the right-wing analysis of America's problems, then we will indeed awaken one morning, and that will, in fact, be a reality. The moderate-liberal community in America, which is supposed to challenge a right-wing analysis, is so busy diving for cover under the banner and safety of right-wing assessment that they have totally abandoned their political responsibility. And many of us on the Left are sitting around waiting for the pendulum to swing from the Right to the Left—as if pendulum swings happened by voodoo, magic, and mysticism.

So tonight is a significant evening. . . .

Whatever has gone before, today the United States is about to initiate a real, significant, awesome, dangerous arms race directed at obtaining a first-strike nuclear capability and necessitating further slashes in human-needs programs to finance it. This is a scary world and we all know it. It is a world with incredibly real problems: the severe economic problems of unemployment, inflation, poverty, resource scarcity, hunger, lack of energy—many real problems and many real threats. But I am absolutely certain that one threat which is *not* real is the alleged possibility of a Soviet nuclear attack on the United States.

California Congressman Ron Dellums addresses over 2000 at public liturgy.

But there *is* another very real threat: that the United States is considering nuclear war a possibility. Once you begin to assume that nuclear war is thinkable, acceptable, possible—as I said earlier—you then move to a point where it becomes inevitable. Many of my colleagues debating on the floor of Congress claim, "We need millions more dollars. To save the American people from a nuclear holocaust, we have to dig holes in the ground." But what the hell do we inherit after somebody drops a nuclear bomb? What's left when you crawl out of the hole? A totally destroyed universe; a totally destroyed earth—that's the scary threat of a nuclear war which might result from our defense policies.

It is postulated by the Right that the Soviet government intends to launch weapons and fight a nuclear war with the United States and the West. They allege that this weakened, cowardly American government is to be overrun by a Soviet megapower, but it just doesn't wash. Let us look at some of the facts. I don't want to give you numbers and just add up how many missiles they have against how many missiles we have, but I will give you some figures in order to make an important point.

The Soviet Union, at this moment, has 4,000 strategic nuclear weapons. The United States has 9,000 strategic nuclear weapons, to say nothing of the 22,000 tactical nuclear weapons. Of our 9,000 strategic nuclear weapons, approximately 5,000 are based on submarines and can be launched from the bottom of the sea, and about half of those 5,000 are always at sea. So tonight, 2,500 of those weapons are on submarines and completely invulnerable for now and the foreseeable future. Whatever the Soviets do, our submarine capability will continue to exist.

Some of the ICBMs and bombers would survive a nuclear attack, but the capability of those invulnerable submarines alone is shuddering to contemplate. For example, about 30 percent of the Soviet population and 50 percent of Soviet industry are located in 100 of their largest cities. Now I want you to think the way Pentagon planners think and understand what those facts mean. The cold, cruel, hard reality is that 400 of the 2,500 of the 5,000 of the 9,000—remember, we started with 9,000 and I broke it down to 5,000 on submarines, with 2,500 on submarines at any given moment—only 400 of our weapons would destroy all 100 Soviet cities.

That capacity to destroy exists in three Poseidon submarines alone, and we have thirty-one of them. Consider the awesome destructive capability that the United States has. These three subs alone would destroy the Soviet Union as a modern society, yet we have a strategic capability of more than twenty times that. "How much is enough?" is the obvious rhetorical question. After all, we can only kill each other once.

First-Strike Capability

In truth, much of our arsenal is at best a waste and at worst the seeds of Armageddon. Since this is not a time when our nuclear deterrent ability is being threatened, why are we hearing these calls for more arms when we already have more arms than we need to destroy ourselves and the rest of the world?

I am convinced that the United States, at this very moment, is attempting to develop a capacity to attack the Soviet Union in a first strike, not facing any retaliatory attack. If this is true, its self-evident effect is staggering. In order for a country to launch a disabling first strike, we would need a missile force capable of destroying enemy missile subs and other hard military targets. It is the MX missile, the Trident II missile, the Mark 12-A and the Mark 500 warheads, combined with new naval systems, which will provide the potential for first-strike nuclear capability.

The resulting combination of increased accuracy, warhead yield, and destructive power is unnecessary for deterrence. They are the basic tools for fighting a nuclear war with options for a first strike or limited nuclear strikes. We have arrived at the utter madness of contemplating a nuclear war, expecting that somehow, in some insane way, life will survive, and that there can indeed be a victor. Yes, this is madness, insanity, cruelty. . . . This is reality.

If there was ever a time for people in this country and throughout the world to stand up and yell—"No more madness! No more bombs! No more missiles! No more war!"—that time is now.

Our weapons are our greatest danger. The plethora of United States forces is a tinderbox. It is up to us now to expose the myth of American capability and its intentions. The post-World-War-II arms race is now more than twenty-five years old. Think about that for a moment. Many of my colleagues on the floor of Congress continue to justify spending billions of dollars to develop more heinous weapons on the grounds that the dangerous Soviet Union is running to build these nuclear weapons. But if you think historically, one nation developed the nuclear capability first, and one nation had the insanity and the audacity to use it—the United States.

In my more cynical moments, I have stopped to ask myself: What would I have done if I had been the leader of a powerful nation looking across the water at the United States, the country which not only had the insanity to build the atomic bomb, but the insanity to drop it? I would have said: "With those fools running rampant in the world, the best thing we can do is build ourselves one too." So we are the leaders in the insanity of nuclear war, not the Soviet Union, and it is important for us to understand that.

A Shift in Priorities

This arms race, which has been going on for twenty-five years, cannot seem to reach clear limits either in quality of weapons, in their spread throughout the world, or in the nature of the weapons. But if the race does not stop, it is hard to see the world remaining free from unprecedented catastrophe for very much longer.

Let me offer this thought: We, the United States, are the unquestioned leader of the arms race; therefore, we are in the best position to stop it—to slow it down. Let the United States unilaterally begin to reduce its weapons.

True, our opponents on the Right will say, "Well, if we begin to reduce our weapons, the Soviet Union will begin to increase theirs." But we can reduce many of our weapons without any real security risk to ourselves, and more important, we will communicate to the world that we are now prepared to back away from the brink of disaster. We are prepared to back away from a journey that will either carry us into economic oblivion or will result in our pushing the button and blowing ourselves off the face of the earth. We choose to back away from that insanity.

Obviously, we know that it cannot be done overnight. But it can be done after challenge, demonstration, and debate have changed the climate of opinion. It can be done step by step, at this military base or that base, in this stockyard or that airfield, in this withheld production or that deferred research. I believe that it is possible for us to call for a halt to the arms race between now and the end of the 1980s, but the dates are less important than the double goals of something real and something soon.

If we are to leave our children a safer and freer world rather than a more dangerous and restricted one, we must change the steady trend in American armaments and world armaments. As the leader in the world's arms race, as the pacesetter for the military and foreign policies of the Western world, the United States has both the responsibility and the opportunity to take the initiative in attempting to shift the fundamental course of global military power.

With respect to priorities, given today's economic and political situation, military spending is the most crucial issue of domestic reform. It is my honest belief that if we continue to place more and more of our resources into a smaller segment of our economy, we will either reach that moment of madness when we will push the button and destroy ourselves, or the economy will fall with the mere weight of the incredibly bloated, wasteful, unnecessary, misguided, and misdirected military budget.

The Military Budget

Remember, the size of the Pentagon budget determines what is left over for everything else, not only in terms of money, but in terms of available talent and political commitment. I find the press often projecting the myth which the Pentagon gives us; namely, that the military budget is 25 percent or less of the total budget. Understand this: Back in the days of Lyndon Baines Johnson, when he tried to hide the billions of dollars we were spending to rain terror on the Vietnamese people in an illegal, immoral, and insane war, he came up with the mechanism known as the unified budget. That means we add together the fixed expenditures of the federal government as well as the general fund revenues, so that the total figure is much larger, thereby reducing the percentage of the military budget.

The American people have come to believe that the unified budget actually reflects what Congress appropriates every year, but the fact of the matter is that approximately 50 percent of that overall budget consists of the federal government's fixed expenditures—sums that we would have to deal with whether or not Congress voted "yea" or "nay" on any proposition. But when you deal with only the amount of money that Congress authorizes, the military budget is 55 percent— that is 55 percent of all the money that the United States Congress appropriates annually, not including fixed expenditures and trust fund revenues. Therefore, if the military budget is sacrosanct, then the rest of the government must wither away, because it would be left with weak, ineffective, underfunded, "knee-jerk" programs which speak only to the symptoms and not the basic causes of human misery and oppression in our country.

While all other government agencies and programs—especially human-needs programs—are scraped to the bone and forced to show efficiency dividends at the expense of significant achievement, only the military maintains its growth at a rate that outstrips inflation. The madness of Proposition 13 is now permeating the American scene, the meanness of spirit that would deny the responsibility of society to deal with human misery. And many of my colleagues voted for 5 percent cuts across-the-board in HEW, the Department of Labor, HUD, and other programs.

But Parren Mitchell, my colleague from Maryland, got up and made an important statement on the floor of Congress, pointing out the incredible contradiction of all my conservative, moderate, and many liberal colleagues who wanted to run home a few weeks ago in order to tell America that they cut the budget. Parren Mitchell got up and said, "I want to see how far you're ready to take Proposition 13," and he offered an amendment to cut one-tenth of 1 percent from the incredible $120 billion military budget.

He got eighty-nine votes, which shows you the mentality of our so-called "leadership" when it comes to cutting the budget and fighting inflation. They only want to fight people who desperately need help. They do not want to fight the dangers that could blow us off the face of the earth. The military budget is untouchable, while the rest of the government withers away.

Our primary task must be to fight against the emphasis on death and destruction which now characterizes the United States government, and to turn this country around to more human possibilities. All our other reforms are doomed to failure if we do not take on the problem of ending the domination of militarism in our political lives. The domestic side of government is being starved to feed the military machine. Nor is this only a problem of government. The Pentagon has first grabs at some of the most important resources of the economy, from energy to scarce technical talent. Pentagon control of the economy represents the largest intrusion of government into the lives of our citizens, anti-welfare rhetoric notwithstanding.

In order to combat the creation of vested interests now protecting the Pentagon, we must submit a large-scale program of economic conversion to a peacetime economy. We can begin to rebuild the cities, which have become monuments to our madness rather than to our sensitivity, brilliance, humanity, and genius. We can begin to say that employment is a right of all people in our country; that education is the right of all people, not a privilege for some; that health care in our society should not be sold in the marketplace the way you sell a Mercedes-Benz or a diamond ring.

The Rights of Americans

There is something immoral and insane about a society that spends $162 billion on health, where the only people reaping any benefit are drug companies, insurance companies, and other wealthy corporations, while tens of thousands of people in our society cannot even afford to be sick in this, the wealthiest nation in the world. I find that contradictory.

What is so radical or so extreme about advocating education as a right; a job as a right; clothing, shelter, food, and health care as rights—the right to a livable community in a livable society? What's so radical or so extreme about that? Opportunities are shrinking in this country and competition is increasing. If we are to avert a holocaust, we must engage in a set of politics capable of expanding opportunities for people.

Right here in New York, the unemployment rate is so high that if I were to offer 10 jobs, paying between $10,000 and $15,000 a year, 10,000 people would show up tomorrow morning. If I were going to interview at 8 A.M., they'd be there by 1 A.M. lined up for those 10 jobs. Of course, if we applied an Affirmative Action test to those 10 jobs, we'd have to hire five men, five women, two blacks, one brown, one red, one yellow, and five whites, and that would take care of our "liberal mentality" with respect to the equity of providing 10 jobs with 10,000 people applying.

As far as I'm concerned, that was the politics of the 1960s and the 1970s, but the politics of the 1980s must answer this question: "What in hell happened to the 9,990 people who went for a job and didn't get one?"

These are the questions we must now begin to raise. We must end the policy of interventionism abroad which has wrecked our own economy while devastating other countries. It is exasperating to hear talk of a trade-off between employment and price stability when the main cause of inflation is not domestic spending, but the cost of past wars, about which successive administrations have never had the nerve to inform us. People have not talked about the incredible inflationary aspects of a bloated and wasteful military budget. People are not talking about the fact that food, health care, energy, and housing are the most inflated items in the economy, so much so that all the working-class people in America spend 70–75 percent of their monthly resources on those four items alone. And you show me where big government spending and union-negotiated contracts inflated the cost of housing, energy, food, and health care. . . . You can't do it.

There is another analysis of America's problems, and if we do not offer it, the right-wing analysis will dominate the American political scene—the analysis that increases military budgets and decreases efforts to solve our human problems. You and I have a profound obligation to enter the arena and to challenge the right-wing, corporate mentality in this country. That mentality cannot capture the American imagination.

I cannot conceive of a nation that has gone through the struggle for civil rights, black liberation, Third-World liberation, women's liberation, gay liberation, senior citizens' liberation, the challenge of the Vietnam War, ecological considerations, and many other social concerns moving further to the Right. But what we are seeing is a small minority of people—well-organized, well-financed, and highly articulate—making that claim, and the tragic reality is that the American media has allowed them to go unchallenged without providing an opportunity for those of us on the Left, and those of us who are the progressives, to challenge that analysis.

Fear permeates the American political system. Fear permeates our thinking on a daily basis: fear of crossing the street, fear of leaving our homes, fear of unlocking our cars, fear of everything. Then we send people to Washington, and we wonder why they are not strong and incredibly courageous people, because they are products of the fear. We catapult people into high political office who have either internalized the fear or who are capable of reflecting the fear.

But it is not frightened, expedience-minded people who will change America and change the world; it is only strong and courageous people. And tonight, we must all join together and be strong, for it is my belief that we *can* bring about a better world.

A Tribute

I always close by paying tribute to a beautiful and prophetic black revolutionary man—the Reverend Dr. Martin Luther King, Jr.— who was eulogized when he died as having been a moderate civil rights leader. But I reject that notion.

He talked about a redistribution of power and a redistribution of wealth when he died, and there was nothing moderate and civil-rightsy about that. He talked about generosity being more than throwing a few crumbs to a beggar; rather, to him it meant dealing with those circumstances inherent in our society that gave rise to the beggar. To me that statement means that it is not "knee-jerk" liberalism which will solve America's problems. It is only when we have the courage to espouse a progressive set of politics based on a humanistic set of values that we will ever right the wrongs and challenge the evils.

Martin Luther King walked on the face of this earth for a short period of time, but in that short period of time he went on an incredibly long journey. He went from Montgomery where he started to Memphis where he died. He went from mere manhood to ultimate martyrdom, and from the depths of misery to the top of the mountain.

If that beautiful and prophetic black man could walk so far in that short period of time, then you and I gathered in this room and in similar places throughout this country—black, brown, red, yellow, and white—can join hands with each other and with people throughout the world struggling for freedom. Together, we can take America and the world on a journey from madness to humanity, from exploitation to equality, from oppression to freedom, and from war to peace. And I humbly join you in that effort.

STRATEGY: WHERE DO WE GO FROM HERE?

Cora Weiss

Thirty-three years ago the United States dropped a bomb on a town and destroyed an area of three square miles, instantly killing 140,000 people. It was an atomic bomb. Three days later another bomb, this one cored with plutonium, killed another 70,000 people. Today we can launch a missile that will destroy 234 square miles and millions of the people living there. We can now destroy twenty-eight Hiroshimas at once with one weapon.

That is why Riverside Church has a program to reverse the arms race. The use of nuclear weapons is not a possibility; it is a fact.

We have just presented you with more facts. You should now be well informed. It would be well if you were also outraged. Our challenge now is to direct that horror in appropriate and effective ways. Unless we all join the race to end the arms race, we can rightly predict the likelihood of war.

We are firmly convinced that we can reverse the arms race. It will take you, your friends, and your communities deeply believing that what we are after—peace—is right and possible. Then we will be required to assume some responsibility for achieving that goal. If we feel responsible for our families, friends, and neighbors, we will do something more than complain. Here are a few of the things we can do.

Let us start with education. The more we know, the more effective we become. We have brought together in this book some of the

CORA WEISS is Director, Riverside Church Disarmament Program.

experts. We urge you to consider the list of further readings. Then we urge you to share that knowledge and your feelings with others. Hold a meeting of your social or civic organization, congregation, or community. Hear testimony from people whose services have been cut back and see where those funds have gone. Do a study of your own town's budget, capital needs, and unmet social services. Find out how many of your tax dollars are returned in services, and how many

Disarmament Program director Cora Weiss unveils "wallposter" campaign. Each poster shows how money that is used for arms could be used for health, education, housing, and other benefits. William Sloane Coffin, Jr., joins in the ceremony.

find their way into defense contracts for plants in other regions. In other words, HOW IS THE PENTAGON DENYING YOUR COMMUNITY JOBS, SERVICES, AND NECESSARY CAPITAL REPAIR AND DEVELOPMENT?

Do you believe that as long as we are first in might but fifteenth in literacy and seventeenth in life expectancy that we can call that national security? Until the Defense and Energy Departments can come up with a budget that provides us with national security and does not threaten the world with war or the cities with economic ruin, we propose that we ask our congressional representatives to vote "no" on the entire military budget. Even if no military funds are voted this year, we still have $75 billion in unexpended weapons procurement funds left over from previous years, at least $20 billion of which are unobligated. An administration official admits that "if the Pentagon figures out how to spend the money it already has, our drive for fiscal stability could go right down the drain."

We urge you to join local efforts aimed at converting military plants to civilian consumer production. For further information on conversion and relevant legislation, write to Senators George McGovern (D—S. Dakota) and Charles Mathias (R—Maryland), Representative Theodore Weiss (D—New York), or SANE (318 Massachusetts Avenue, Washington, DC 20002).

Your own church can take the initiative in urging your denomination to join others in supporting a resolution to reverse the arms race, establishing a full-time office on disarmament, and publishing articles on this issue in religious periodicals.

Do General Electric, Sperry Rand, General Dynamics, or other weapons manufacturers have offices or facilities in your area? Ask for a meeting with their management to find out what they are doing. How safe is your town if they produce nuclear weapons? Do the workers realize the connection between their jobs and war, or the economy? Do they realize there could be more jobs if consumer goods were produced?

Join demonstrations protesting the use of your tax dollars for militarism instead of city services and human needs.

Write to your congressional representatives, urging them to vote "no" on legislation calling for youths to register as a first step toward reinstating the Draft. No just war can be fought today; therefore no Draft is necessary.

The important thing is that we all continue to raise our voices and join hands in challenging the military-industrial complex, whose efforts are preventing the fruitful expression of life.

SUGGESTIONS FOR FURTHER READING

BOOKS

Anderson, M., *The Empty Pork Barrel.* Public Interest Research Group (615 E. Michigan Avenue, Lansing, MI 48933), April, 1975.

Barnet, Richard J., *Roots of War.* New York: Penguin Books, Inc. 1971.

Barnet, Richard J., *The Giants: Russia and America.* New York: Simon & Schuster, Inc., 1977.

Boston Study Group, *The Price of Defense: A New Strategy for Military Spending.* New York: Times Books, div. of The New York Times Book Co., 1978. (Authors include Martin Moore-Ede, Randall Forsberg, Philip Morrison, Phylis Morrison, Paul F. Walker, George Sommaripa.)

Caldicott, Helen, *Nuclear Madness, What You Can Do.* Brookline: Autumn Press, 1978.

Defense Economy: Conversion of Industries and Occupations to Civilian Needs, a series in six volumes, Seymour Melman, editor. New York: Praeger Publishers, Inc., 1970.
The volumes:
Conversion of Military-Oriented Research and Development to Civilian Uses, Marvin Berkowitz;
Conversion of Nuclear Facilities from Military to Civilian Uses: A Case Study in Hanford, Washington, Aris Christodoulou;
Civilian Markets for Military-Electronics Ind., J. Ullmann;
Conversion of Shipbuilding from Military to Civilian Markets, Daniel Mack-Forlist and Arthur Newman;

Local Economic Development after Military Base Closures,
John E. Lynch;

The Defense Economy, Seymour Melman, ed.

The Economic Impact of Reductions in Defense Spending (A summary of research prepared for the U.S. Arms Control and Disarmament Agency), Washington, D.C: Publication #64, U.S. Government Printing Office, July 1, 1972.

Fitzgerald, A. Ernest, *The High Priests of Waste.* New York: W.W. Norton & Co., Inc., 1972.

Fox, J. Ronald, *Arming America: How the U.S. Buys Weapons.* Cambridge: Harvard University Press, 1974.

Johansen, Robert C., *The Disarmament Process: Where to Begin.* New York: Institute for World Order (1140 Avenue of the Americas, NY 10036), 1977.

Klare, Michael, *War Without End: American Planning for the Next Vietnams.* New York: Vintage Books, Inc., div. of Random House, 1972.

Lens, Sidney, *The Day Before Doomsday: An Anatomy of the Nuclear Arms Race.* New York: Doubleday & Co., Inc., 1977.

Melman, Seymour, *Our Depleted Society.* New York: Holt, Rinehart and Winston (also Dell Paperbacks, 1966), 1965.

Melman, Seymour, *Planning for Conversion of Military-Industrial and Military Base Facilities.* U.S. Dept. of Commerce, Economic Development Administration, Office of Technical Assistance, 1973.

Melman, Seymour, *The Permanent War Economy.* New York: Simon & Schuster, Inc., 1974.

Melman, Seymour, *The War Economy of the United States: Readings in Military Industry and Economy.* New York: St. Martin's Press, Inc., 1971.

Ravenal, Earl C., *Never Again: Learning from America's Foreign Policy Failures.* Philadelphia: Temple University Press, 1978.

Transnational Institute for Policy Studies (1901 Que Street, N.W., Washington, DC 20009). A series of five publications:

Aldridge, Robert C., *The Counter Force Syndrome: A Guide to U.S. Nuclear Weapons and Strategic Doctrine;*

Kaplan, Fred M., *Dubious Specter: A Second Look at the Soviet Threat;*

Klare, Michael, *Resurgent Militarism;*

Klare, Michael, and Holland, Max, *Conventional Arms Restraint: An Unfulfilled Promise;*

Ravenal, Earl C., *Toward World Security: A Program for Disarmament.*

U.S. Department of Labor, Bureau of Labor Statistics., *Productivity and the Economy* (Bulletin # 1710). Washington, D.C., 1971.

Yoder, John Howard, *The Politics of Jesus.* Grand Rapids: Wm. B. Eerdmans Publishing Company, 1972.

ARTICLES AND REPORTS

Aronsan, Robert, "Effect of Federal Spending on Scientists and Engineers," *Monthly Labor Review,* vol. 93 (October, 1970).

Barnet, Richard, "Challenging the Myths of National Security," *The New York Times Magazine* (April 1, 1979), p. 25.

Cambern, J. R., and Newton, D. A., "Skill Transfers: Can Defense Workers Adapt to Civilian Occupations?" *Monthly Labor Review,* vol. 92 (June, 1969).

Council on Economic Priorities (84 Fifth Avenue, New York, NY 10011):

"CEP's Conversion Information Center" (1979 Newsletter);

Duffy, Gloria, and Adams, Gordon, "Power Politics—The Nuclear Industry and Nuclear Exports" (1978);

Edelstein, Michael, "Economic Impact of Military Spending" (1977);

Lydenberg, Steven, "Weapons for the World/Update II" (1978);

"The Defense Department's Top 100" (CEP Annual Newsletter).

Dumas, L. J., "Economic Conversion, Productive Efficiency and Social Welfare," *Journal of Sociology and Social Welfare* (Jan.–March, 1977).

Holloman, J., and Harger, A., "America's Technological Dilemma," *Technology Review* (July–Aug., 1971).

Melman, Seymour, "Decision Making and Productivity as Economic Variables: The Present Depression as a Failure of Productivity," *Journal of Economic Issues* (June, 1976).

Melman, Seymour, "Beating 'Swords' into Subways," *The New York Times Magazine* (November 19, 1978), p. 43.

Melman, Seymour, "Inflation and Unemployment as Products of War Economy," *Bulletin of Peace Proposals,* vol. 9, no. 4 (1978).

"The Arms Race and Our Souls," special issue of *Christianity and Crisis,* vol. 38, no. 18 (Nov. 27, 1978).

Articles include:

Barnet, Richard J., "The Myth of Power, the Power of Myth";

Bennett, John C., "The Disarmament Cause: Priorities and Puzzles";

Coffin, William Sloane, Jr., "Dealing with the Devil: A Cost Benefit Analysis";

Dumas, Lloyd J., "Why Buying Guns Raises the Price of Our Butter";
Lekachman, Robert, "Why Our Congress Buys Guns Anyway."